SINGING
SCHOOL

SINGING

LEARNING TO WRITE (AND READ) POETRY

SCHOOL

BY STUDYING WITH THE MASTERS

ROBERT PINSKY

W. W. NORTON & COMPANY · New York · LONDON

For information about special discounts for bulk purchases, please contact
W. W. Norton Special Sales at specialsales@wwnorton.com or 800-233-4830

Manufacturing by Courier Westford
Book design by JAM Design
Production manager: Louise Mattarelliano

Library of Congress Cataloging-in-Publication Data

Pinsky, Robert.
Singing school : learning to write (and read) poetry by studying with the masters /
Robert Pinsky. — First edition.
pages cm
Includes bibliographical references and index.
ISBN 978-0-393-05068-4 (hardcover)
1. Poetry—Authorship. 2. Poetry—Appreciation. 3. Poetics. I. Title.
PN1059.A9P56 2013
808.1—dc23
2013022146

W. W. Norton & Company, Inc.
500 Fifth Avenue, New York, N.Y. 10110
www.wwnorton.com

W. W. Norton & Company Ltd.
Castle House, 75/76 Wells Street, London W1T 3QT

1 2 3 4 5 6 7 8 9 0

CONTENTS

IV. DREAMING THINGS UP / 145

PREFACE

I HAVE HEARD ALLEN Ginsberg recite John Milton's "Lycidas" from memory. Ginsberg possibly could thank his poet father, or his teachers at Columbia University, for calling "Lycidas" to his attention, but he absorbed and recalled its music for his own purposes, by his own judgment. Ginsberg's notebooks, with their self-set exercises in iambic pentameter, demonstrate the process. (With a serious student's requisite combination of compliance and resistance, the apprentice Ginsberg forms a correct pentameter line on his own subject: "Let cockcrow crown the buttocks of my Pete.")

That the poem by Milton (1608–1674) had gotten under the skin of Ginsberg (1926–1997) exemplifies the ideas that govern this book: examples precede analysis; young poets can learn a lot from old poetry. Models provide inspiration, which is different from imitation. The visual artist looks at the world, but also at art. Similarly, the musician listens, the cook eats, the athlete watches great athletes, the filmmaker watches great movies, in order to gain mastery from examples.

In an interview that begins the CD album *American Classic*, the great tenor saxophonist Dexter Gordon is asked the question any aspiring artist might put to an eminent master:

"Where do you get your inspiration?"

The first two words out of Dexter's mouth are: "Lester Young." Then he names Billie Holiday and the Ellington Band. He continues, with a concise, accurate statement of what it means to be an artist, the source of his inspiration: "The music that thrilled me when I was young . . . still thrills me. I remember the feeling it gave me, and I want to give other people that feeling."

In "Sailing to Byzantium," William Butler Yeats makes a similar statement:

Nor is there singing school but studying
Monuments of its own magnificence.

In his first draft, as recorded in *The Variorum Edition*, Yeats made his declaration even more definitive:

And there's no singing school but studying
Monuments of its own magnificence.

If you want to learn singing, you must study—not just peruse or experience or dabble in or enjoy or take a course in, but *study*—monumental examples of magnificent singing: study not just a pretty good poem in a recent magazine, or something that seems cool or seems to be in fashion, or that you have been taught in school, but examples that you feel are *magnificent*. "Magni-ficent": the Latin roots of the word mean "making great."

A reasonable question: "Who decides what is magnificent? Who says what is a monument? Who chooses?" The answer is implicit in Dexter Gordon's remarks: *you* do: the aspirant, the true student, the passionate reader inspired to write, chooses. No curriculum or official canon will suffice: the examples must proceed from what thrills each person. I give my examples here, hoping each reader will do the same: specific works chosen by an individual reader (me), the poems here are examples *of examples*.

For me, this anthology will succeed if it encourages the reader to emulate it by replacing it, or supplementing it: create your own anthology by typing out the writing that inspires you. Save the models you select in a computer file that might be called

"Anthology," or in a different traditional term "Daybook." Each reader's own personal anthology could even be created, in part, by cutting-and-pasting from websites—that would be better than nothing. But actually typing the poem at a keyboard is the most effective method. Typing a poem, one memorizes it a few words at a time, sometimes one syllable at a time. Every word gets read. By hitting the Return key at the end of each typographical line, one might learn something about the poetic line. The physical act of typing the poem can reinforce the act of judgment that selected it.

The work of making a personal anthology, searching, studying, and selecting—whether literally making it as a computer file to print out, or virtually making it as one's mental canon of essential poems—is demanding and lifelong. It is no wonder that many prefer some easier course, such as those offered by the turning wheel of trends: be confessional, or be postmodern, or be formalist, or be imagistic, or become an adherent of some literal or figurative school, or model yourself on your university teachers, or pay close attention to your most successful peers. These are fatally easy ways to avoid the double labor of deciding for yourself what thrills you and studying it. And sometimes changing your mind.

The path I suggest is stringent, and I don't mean to exclude help in following it. The testimony of experts, scholars, anthologists, can be useful: "I knew *Palgrave's Golden Treasury* by heart," says William Carlos Williams of himself as a young poet, sorting out what he thought was magnificent, and what was not, in that immensely popular anthology of his youth. His taste is not visible in the *Golden Treasury*, but his course toward his taste perhaps is.

Does this anthology, then, suggest a *literary* approach to poetry? Yes, indeed it does, though I might prefer to call it a technical approach. It resembles taking a musical approach to music, a culinary approach to cooking, an athletic approach to basketball, a cinematic approach to moviemaking.

Or to look at it another way, a deep knowledge of the art can free one from being "literary" in the pejorative sense. The writing I did early in my life, when I knew very little, was quite old-fashioned, literary in a way I inhaled like an invisible gas, vaguely, from the culture. The more I read, the less literary my writing became.

A GUIDE LIKE this book aims to make useful hints and suggestions for the journey. The organizing principles and examples I offer are more or less arbitrary, rather than pretending to be definitive. All the examples could be used to illustrate other principles, and the principles could be illustrated by other examples. Another time, I might choose different poems and formulate different chapter divisions. My careful effort has been to offer some models for a quest that each serious student of poetry must create anew—as a personal, unique adventure. My introductions and headnotes are brief because the great work and the great adventure belong to the student, not me. I have tried to give hints about the principles and openings the poems suggest to me.

Instead of the standard textbook structure with "Assignments," "Further Exercises," "Questions About the Text," "Suggestions for Further Study," etc., I find it more congenial, and maybe more in the spirit of art, to make occasional suggestions in the headnotes to the poems: not assignments so much as examples of assignments that clever students might want to make for themselves. Imagining an assignment might be a first step to imagining a poem.

I emphasize historical examples partly because historical models can ensure that the student will not be merely imitative. It takes creative effort to learn from a poem by Ben Jonson or Emily Dickinson, discovering an essence, beyond a manner. A further benefit is that the old poem can provide, as well as a useful model, a useful limitation: precisely because their English language is that of the seventeenth or nineteenth century, not the twenty-first, you are not likely to parrot the voices of Jonson or Dickinson. You probably will not just ape their moves in some superficial way, as might happen with a contemporary. Ginsberg learned from Milton, but he did not write like Milton.

The four section headings and their order, though not exhaustive, do represent essentials. "Freedom" is where the artist begins: there are no rules, and the principles and habits are up to you. Having confronted and embraced freedom, the poet engages the particular work of "Listening": sentences have melodic patterns of pitch, as well as cadences, and great work can help you hear them. So too can the speech you hear every day. The third section uses the word "Form" in a sense related to form in dance or sports—the effective shapes and arrangements of energy—rather than particular "forms" and their required patterns. Finally, "Dreaming Things Up" affirms that many essential and thrilling elements of poetry have to do with what cannot be explained: something new, waking life transformed.

To emphasize vocality, the sound of the language in an actual voice, I have limited myself mainly to poems written in English. To emphasize the depth of the past, and incidentally to avoid squabbles and prejudices, I have excluded living contemporaries. The book is brief rather than fat for many reasons: one is portability; another is my conviction that the best anthology is the one each reader compiles, personally, according to his or her judgment, pleasure, and awe.

I have tried to give memorable examples of poetry, choices guided by the vital unity of writing and reading.

I

FREEDOM

THERE ARE NO rules.

Or, you can modify that rule by observing that each work of art generates its own unique rules. Consider the exchanges in Frank O'Hara's poem "Why I Am Not a Painter" (p. 12). O'Hara sees that his friend Mike Goldberg is working on a painting that contains the letters SARDINES.

"You have SARDINES in it," says the poet.

"Yes, it needed something there," the painter responds in O'Hara's poem: "It needed something there."

After a time, O'Hara returns to the studio, the painting has been finished. "Where's SARDINES?" asks the poet, seeing that "All that's left is just / letters."

"'It was too much,' Mike says."

Impulses, swerves, collisions, flights, descents, gags, indirections, surprises, exploding cigars, non sequiturs: all are allowed or encouraged, and all in some sense begin to create their own principles.

There are no rules, but uniformity in art can make it feel as though there are rules: the more unconscious or unperceived (as with widely accepted fashions), the more confining.

A reigning style can feel tyrannical: the assumptions behind it so well-established that there seem to be no alternatives. But there are always alternatives. How might a resourceful, ambitious artist get past or around a perceived tyranny? European painters early in the twentieth century, challenging the academic norm, found something useful in Japanese cigarette papers and African masks.

The past can offer a useful way of rebelling against the orthodoxies of the present. The early modernist poets revived interest in John Donne and Andrew Marvell, not because they wanted to correct the academic reading lists—that was a side effect—but because they were impatient with late-late Romantic, post-Victorian softness. They craved models of hard-edged intelligence and lightning wit.

In the 1970s, a young poet I knew described the manner most prevalent in the magazines and writing workshops of those days as "just grooving on images." I remember that poet—now a considerable and innovative figure—introducing me to James Shirley's "The Glories of Our Blood and State" (p. 32), praising the poem for the force of its statement and idiom, the cogency of its propositions, and its cadences. Those elements carried along the effectively minimal imagery: swords and laurels and breath, even the conventional "icy hand" of death.

James Shirley's lyric had another virtue to offer poets in the 1970s: the seventeenth-century form and idiom, nearly everything about the poem, made it impossible to simply imitate. Today, young poets might imitate my friend or Frank O'Hara (many do) but they could not possibly imitate James Shirley, any more than Picasso merely made African masks. Remote models require assimilation. You can learn from the past with little risk of merely aping it as you might ape your contemporaries, or the generation just before your own.

A young poet impatient with the assumptions and styles of the present might look for springboards and encouragements in another time.

In "The Old Cloak" (p. 16), an anonymous ballad from the sixteenth century, the wife brings in, from beyond left field, King Stephen and his virtues. That's when you know the argument has been won. Or maybe you know it the moment she mentions their livestock: "I'll have a new cloak about me," he says, and she begins her response with a devastating combination of non sequitur and stubborn emphasis, "Cow Crumbock is a very good cow."

Like many comedy writers, this poet of five hundred years ago likes to slip in an extra gag here and there. When Bell the wife mentions that they have had between them either nine children or ten, is it uncertain memory, or uncertain paternity? As with similar arbitrary-looking, incidental-seeming jokes written for *The Simpsons* or *Curb Your Enthusiasm*, the freedom—the implicit right to pause or digress or hurry—is part of the point. The writer claims the puppeteer's liberty to wink at the reader above his creatures—in a sense, becoming one of his creatures. The work's freedom to establish its own unique principles, alive in particular cadences and words and lines and sentences: that is the goal.

"The Old Cloak" contains old, unfamiliar words. I will not outright forbid the student to look up "threap" from the last stanza or "flyte" from the second stanza. But the most promising poetry student will skip along, relishing the unfamiliarity and the sounds, confident in the meanings that emerge from context, sound, smell. The husband says about his old cloak: "It is so bare and over worn / A crickè thereon cannot renn." If you cannot figure out what a "crickè" might be and what it means for a crickè to "renn," perhaps you need to reread Lewis Carroll's "Jabberwocky" (p. 183).

Serious students of poetry should use the dictionary to look up familiar words: words you know the meaning of already, so you can learn more about them. Also, learn to take the unfamiliar words for their feel and aroma, leaving the dictionary for later. For example, "apparell" is quite familiar in the modern spelling "apparel," a specialized or stuffy contemporary term: a retail word, with some old-fashioned overtone of classiness. *Apparel* is more expensive or special than *clothes*. (*Clothing* somewhere in between?) That is pretty much how *He* in "The Old Cloak" uses it: "For once I'll new apparell'd be."

But if you look the word up—nearly at random, for no good reason, with no necessity—you discover that behind the Middle

English origin meaning "to make ready or fit" lies the Old French *aparellier*, which is in turn based on the Latin *ad* meaning "to" in a sense of "change to" plus *par* meaning "equal." Related to the term "par" in golf, and to "parity": dressed equal to an occasion. Lurking deep in "For once I'll new apparell'd be" is the high-class or learned quality of Latin, along with the idea of being or making oneself equal, or socially correct: notions and overtones interesting to muse on in relation to this old poem about the two sexes and about poor peasants, with the poem clearly written by someone of education as well as wit.

Such musings about "apparell" are possibly useful, and possibly useless: tendrils of meaning, alive and sprawling in the sounds of words. Uncountable, each sprouting from a bit of language, they express the freedom of poetry. For the poet, the dictionary is not an alphabetical bagful of equations, but a provisional account of meanings as live organisms. With meaning, as with its conjoined twin nonsense, nothing is pure. That is, in "nonsense" any particular made-up word or syllable will connote something; in "sense," any actual word includes, along with its meanings and shades of meaning, an element of the arbitrary grunt.

The aspiring poet should read historical poetry partly by feel, not necessarily using a dictionary or glossary like a tourist with a phrase book. The intrepid traveler can learn by listening to the language, eagerly alert to context. Lewis Carroll's great example of these principles, "Jabberwocky" (p. 183), was originally published (first stanza only, with eccentric typography) as "Stanza of Anglo-Saxon Poetry":

> 'Twas brillig, and the slithy toves
> Did gyre and gimble in the wabe:
> All mimsy were the borogoves,
> And the mome raths outgrabe.

This demonstration of how sound and context make things clear appears in *Through the Looking-Glass*, where Alice brings it for elucidation to the literary critic Humpty Dumpty, who explains, "I can explain all the poems that ever were invented—and a good many that haven't been invented just yet." As is true with many critics, the Dumpty explanations are both ingenious and ponderous.

Another kind of freedom is embodied in movement and change, sometimes sudden: the second half of a poem contrasting with the first, as in Walter Ralegh's "Nature, That Washed Her Hands in Milk" (p. 100):

Nature, that washed her hands in milk
And had forgot to dry them,
Instead of earth took snow and silk
At Love's request, to try them
If she a mistress could compose
To please Love's fancy out of those.

Her eyes he would should be of light,
A violet breath, and lips of jelly,
Her hair not black nor over-bright,
And of the softest down her belly:
As for her inside, he'd have it
Only of wantonness and wit.

At Love's entreaty, such a one
Nature made, but with her beauty
She hath framed a heart of stone,
So as Love, by ill destiny,
Must die for her whom Nature gave him,
Because her darling would not save him.

But Time, which Nature doth despise,
And rudely gives her love the lie,
Makes hope a fool and sorrow wise,
His hands doth neither wash nor dry,

But, being made of steel and rust,
Turns snow and silk and milk to dust.

The light, the belly, lips and breath,
He dims, discolors, and destroys,
With those he feeds (but fills not) Death
Which sometimes were the food of Joys:
Yea, Time doth dull each lively wit,
And dries all wantonness with it.

O cruel Time, which takes in trust
Our youth, our joys, and all we have,
And pays us but with age and dust;
Who in the dark and silent grave,
When we have wandered all our ways,
Shuts up the story of our days.

The poem wheels abruptly from something pretty and conventional to something quite different. How does Walter Ralegh do it? Probably without needing to think about it—second nature, technique, which is to say talent developed by practice. Descriptive analysis of technique, as in sports or music, laboriously breaks down into parts actions that in reality are fluid and momentary.

But slowing down to analyze details can be useful. Like athletes watching video, breaking a fluid action down into its objective parts, we can note, early in the poem, polysyllabic words, light accents, and sentences that pour across the lines:

Instead of earth took snow and silk
At Love's request, to try them
If she a mistress could compose
To please Love's fancy out of those.

The third line, for example, with its two two-syllable words, with the third accent (on "could") relatively light, rather than markedly heavier than the unaccented "-tress"; the sentences rushing across from line to line rather than stopping at the rhymes: these contribute to a rapid, dancing movement.

In contrast—putting meaning aside, quite apart from anything the poem says—in the second half of the poem there are more one-syllable words; the difference between accented syllables and unaccented syllables is much more distinct; the grammatical units are shorter, with end-stopped lines: all making the movement slower, more ponderous:

Makes hope a fool and sorrow wise,
His hands doth neither wash nor dry,
But, being made of steel and rust,
Turns snow and silk and milk to dust.

The final line of the stanza exemplifies the slower movement and elements that produce it: the eight one-syllable words; the four distinct, heavy accents; the end-of-line pauses on the rhymes "rust" and "dust."

Studying these elements in Ralegh's rhymed, metrical poem might help the perceptive student attain a more various, sensitive movement even in less metrical forms. To study what Ralegh does, the ways he changes the lengths of words, the treatment of the line, the degree of accent, is instructive at a primary and significant level. Technical matters, like the fingering of a difficult passage in music, merit respect.

But that is only part of it. At a deeper level, it is worth pondering the mysterious confidence—or is it impatience with the conventions of love poetry he summons to begin his poem?—that leads Ralegh to make something unexpected. He manages to convey pleasure in conventional material, like praising the lady's parts with metaphors ("violet breath and lips of jelly"), even while implicitly mocking its absurdity—mortality and absurdity emphasizing and reinforcing one another.

Explanation always falls short of such vital elements. Extravagant yet systematic, berserk yet purposeful, the mysterious anonymous poem "The Man of Double Deed" (p. 000) fulfills the doubleness of its own title—the poem itself is of double deed:

> There was a man of double deed,
> Who sowed his garden full of seed;
> When the seed began to grow,
> 'Twas like a garden full of snow;
> When the snow began to melt,
> 'Twas like a ship without a belt;
> When the ship began to sail,
> 'Twas like a bird without a tail;
> When the bird began to fly,
> 'Twas like an eagle in the sky;
> When the sky began to roar,
> 'Twas like a lion at my door;
> When my door began to crack,
> 'Twas like a stick across my back;
> When my back began to smart,
> 'Twas like a penknife in my heart;
> And when my heart began to bleed,
> 'Twas death, and death, and death indeed.

After all of the doubles, promised at the outset, there's a thrilling force to the triple repetition of "death" at the end. And after all of the weird, increasingly sinister, and complicated leaps from thing to thing, and rhyme to rhyme, there's a tremendous finality to the simplicity of death: an unrhymed one-syllable word and death indeed.

"The Man of Double Deed" generates a unique feeling with its extreme, dark narrative system. The difference between system and logic is the difference between that poem and John Wilmot's equally intense and strange "Upon Nothing" (p. 70). Wilmot's logic-chopping ingenuity, in a way linear, lets him roam through a dizzy catalogue of savageries, jokes, and rages.

In both cases, the poetic energy exhilarates, with a momentum beyond paraphrase.

A poem is free, and it shows its freedom by establishing its own principles: the unique physics and chemistry and atmosphere of a new planet. From a new planet where Time turns snow and silk and milk to dusk, or where the sky roars like a lion at my door, or where a meditation "On Nothing" is clinched with observations about national characters, kings, whores, and great men—the familiar world can be seen in a new way.

Poetry like ice-skating or fast-break basketball. Not wading.
Make a title beginning with "How" or "Three Ways That . . ."
or some such implied promise, and then in your poem that fol-
lows break or defy the promise, or complicate it.

Why I Am Not a Painter

I am not a painter, I am a poet.
Why? I think I would rather be
a painter, but I am not. Well,

for instance, Mike Goldberg
is starting a painting. I drop in.
"Sit down and have a drink" he
says. I drink; we drink. I look
up. "You have SARDINES in it."
"Yes, it needed something there."
"Oh." I go and the days go by
and I drop in again. The painting
is going on, and I go, and the days
go by. I drop in. The painting is
finished. "Where's SARDINES?"
All that's left is just
letters, "It was too much," Mike says.

But me? One day I am thinking of
a color: orange. I write a line
about orange. Pretty soon it is a
whole page of words, not lines.
Then another page. There should be
so much more, not of orange, of
words, of how terrible orange is

and life. Days go by. It is even in
prose, I am a real poet. My poem
is finished and I haven't mentioned
orange yet. It's twelve poems, I call
it ORANGES. And one day in a gallery
I see Mike's painting, called SARDINES.

MICHELANGELO, "On Painting the Sistine Chapel Ceiling"
(translated by Gail Mazur)

The great painter and sculptor was also a serious, gifted poet.
Possibly a sense of his actual, great skills and accomplishments
gave him the freedom to conclude his gloriously sour complaint
by saying "I am not a painter"?

Michelangelo: To Giovanni da Pistoia When the Author Was
Painting the Vault of the Sistine Chapel

1509

I've already grown a goiter from this torture,
hunched up here like a cat in Lombardy
(or anywhere else where the stagnant water's poison).
My stomach's squashed under my chin, my beard's
pointing at heaven, my brain's crushed in a casket,
my breast twists like a harpy's. My brush,
above me all the time, dribbles paint
so my face makes a fine floor for droppings!

My haunches are grinding into my guts,
my poor ass strains to work as a counterweight,
every gesture I make is blind and aimless.
My skin hangs loose below me, my spine's
all knotted from folding over itself.
I'm bent taut as a Syrian bow.

Because I'm stuck like this, my thoughts
area crazy, perfidious tripe:
anyone shoots badly through a crooked blowpipe.

My painting is dead.
Defend it for me, Giovanni, protect my honor.
I am not in the right place—I am not a painter.

The cat with the shoelace of mouse tail dangling from his jaws:
no reasonable interpretation can entirely explain it away. A
mysterious confidence and autonomy, a creature freedom,
remains. Worth trying: the abstract word for a title; the unex-
pected dictum quoted from an unexpected character; the enig-
matic, playful-ominous image; the snap of wit at the end. Or
maybe, those elements but in a different order?

Silence

My father used to say,
"Superior people never make long visits,
have to be shown Longfellow's grave
or the glass flowers at Harvard.
Self-reliant like the cat—
that takes its prey to privacy,
the mouse's limp tail hanging like a shoelace from its mouth—
they sometimes enjoy solitude,
and can be robbed of speech
by speech which has delighted them.
The deepest feeling always shows itself in silence;
not in silence, but restraint."
Nor was he insincere in saying, "Make my house your inn."
Inns are not residences.

ANONYMOUS, "The Old Cloak"

You know that the wife is in control of the discussion when she begins with an apparent non sequitur: "King Stephen was a very good king."

The Old Cloak

16th century(?)

> This winter's weather it waxeth cold,
>   And frost it freezeth on every hill,
> And Boreas blows his blast so bold
>   That all our cattle are like to spill.
> Bell, my wife, she loves no strife;
>   She said unto me quietlye,
> Rise up, and save cow Crumbock's life!
>   Man, put thine old cloak about thee!
>
> He. O Bell my wife, why dost thou flyte?
>   Thou kens my cloak is very thin:
> It is so bare and over worn,
>   A crickè thereon cannot renn.
> Then I'll no longer borrow nor lend;
>   For once I'll new apparell'd be;
> To-morrow I'll to town and spend;
>   For I'll have a new cloak about me.
>
> She. Cow Crumbock is a very good cow:
>   She has been always true to the pail;
> She has helped us to butter and cheese, I trow,
>   And other things she will not fail.
> I would be loth to see her pine.
>   Good husband, counsel take of me:

It is not for us to go so fine—
    Man, take thine old cloak about thee!

He. My cloak it was a very good cloak,
    It hath been always true to the wear;
But now it is not worth a groat:
    I have had it four and forty year'.
Sometime it was of cloth in grain:
    'Tis now but a sigh clout, as you may see:
It will neither hold out wind nor rain;
    And I'll have a new cloak about me.

She. It is four and forty years ago
    Sine the one of us the other did ken;
And we have had, betwixt us two,
    Of children either nine or ten:
We have brought them up to women and men:
    In the fear of God I trow they be.
And why wilt thou thyself misken?
    Man, take thine old cloak about thee!

He. O Bell my wife, why dost thou flyte?
    Now is now, and then was then:
Seek now all the world throughout,
    Thou kens not clowns from gentlemen:
They are clad in black, green, yellow and blue,
    So far above their own degree.
Once in my life I'll take a view;
    For I'll have a new cloak about me.

She. King Stephen was a worthy peer;
    His breeches cost him but a crown;
He held them sixpence all too dear,
    Therefore he called the tailor 'lown.'
He was a king and wore the crown,

And thou'se but of a low degree:
It's pride that puts this country down:
Man, take thy old cloak about thee!

He. Bell my wife, she loves not strife,
     Yet she will lead me, if she can;
And to maintain an easy life
     I oft must yield, though I'm good-man.
It's not for a man with a woman to threap,
     Unless he first give o'er the plea:
As we began, so will we keep,
     And I'll take my old cloak about me.

The free-swinging language lets him express his mixed, ambiv-
alent yearning toward ordinary, standard-issue life, along with
his loathing for it. He enjoys inventing those inappropriate sur-
real phrases, each a celebration and demonstration of freedom.

Marriage

Should I get married? Should I be good?
Astound the girl next door with my velvet suit and faustus
    hood?
Don't take her to movies but to cemeteries
tell all about werewolf bathtubs and forked clarinets
then desire her and kiss her and all the preliminaries
and she going just so far and I understanding why
not getting angry saying You must feel! It's beautiful to feel!
Instead take her in my arms lean against an old crooked
    tombstone
and woo her the entire night the constellations in the sky—

When she introduces me to her parents
back straightened, hair finally combed, strangled by a tie,
should I sit knees together on their 3rd degree sofa
and not ask Where's the bathroom?
How else to feel other than I am,
often thinking Flash Gordon soap—
O how terrible it must be for a young man
seated before a family and the family thinking
We never saw him before! He wants our Mary Lou!
After tea and homemade cookies they ask What do you do
    for a living?

Should I tell them? Would they like me then?
Say All right get married, we're losing a daughter

but we're gaining a son—
And should I then ask Where's the bathroom?

O God, and the wedding! All her family and her friends
and only a handful of mine all scroungy and bearded
just wait to get at the drinks and food—
And the priest! he looking at me as if I masturbated
asking me Do you take this woman for your lawful wedded
    wife?
And I trembling what to say say Pie Glue!
I kiss the bride all those corny men slapping me on the back
She's all yours, boy! Ha-ha-ha!
And in their eyes you could see some obscene honeymoon
    going on—
Then all that absurd rice and clanky cans and shoes
Niagara Falls! Hordes of us! Husbands! Wives! Flowers!
    Chocolates!
All streaming into cozy hotels
All going to do the same thing tonight
The indifferent clerk he knowing what was going to happen
The lobby zombies they knowing what
The whistling elevator man he knowing
The winking bellboy knowing
Everybody knowing! I'd be almost inclined not to do anything!
Stay up all night! Stare that hotel clerk in the eye!
Screaming: I deny honeymoon! I deny honeymoon!
running rampant into those almost climactic suites
yelling Radio belly! Cat shovel!
O I'd live in Niagara forever! in a dark cave beneath the Falls
I'd sit there the Mad Honeymooner
devising ways to break marriages, a scourge of bigamy
a saint of divorce—

But I should get married I should be good
How nice it'd be to come home to her

and sit by the fireplace and she in the kitchen
aproned young and lovely wanting my baby
and so happy about me she burns the roast beef
and comes crying to me and I get up from my big papa chair
saying Christmas teeth! Radiant brains! Apple deaf!
God what a husband I'd make! Yes, I should get married!
So much to do! like sneaking into Mr. Jones' house late at night
and cover his golf clubs with 1920 Norwegian books
Like hanging a picture of Rimbaud on the lawnmower
like pasting Tannu Tuva postage stamps all over the picket
    fence
like when Mrs. Kindhead comes to collect for the Community
    Chest
grab her and tell her There are unfavorable omens in the sky!
And when the mayor comes to get my vote tell him
When are you going to stop people killing whales!
And when the milkman comes leave him a note in the bottle
Penguin dust, bring me penguin dust, I want penguin dust—

Yet if I should get married and it's Connecticut and snow
and she gives birth to a child and I am sleepless, worn,
up for nights, head bowed against a quiet window, the past
    behind me,
finding myself in the most common of situations a trembling
    man knowledged with responsibility not twig-smear nor
    Roman coin soup—
O what would that be like!
Surely I'd give it for a nipple a rubber Tacitus
For a rattle a bag of broken Bach records
Tack Della Francesca all over its crib
Sew the Greek alphabet on its bib
And build for its playpen a roofless Parthenon

No, I doubt I'd be that kind of father
not rural not snow no quiet window

but hot smelly tight New York City
seven flights up, roaches and rats in the walls
a fat Reichian wife screeching over potatoes Get a job!
And five nose running brats in love with Batman
And the neighbors all toothless and dry haired
like those hag masses of the 18th century
all wanting to come in and watch TV
The landlord wants his rent
Grocery store Blue Cross Gas & Electric Knights of Columbus
Impossible to lie back and dream Telephone snow, ghost
    parking—
No! I should not get married I should never get married!
But—imagine If I were married to a beautiful sophisticated
    woman
tall and pale wearing an elegant black dress and long black
    gloves
holding a cigarette holder in one hand and a highball in the
    other
and we lived high up in a penthouse with a huge window
from which we could see all of New York and ever farther on
    clearer days
No, can't imagine myself married to that pleasant prison
    dream—

O but what about love? I forget love
not that I am incapable of love
it's just that I see love as odd as wearing shoes—
I never wanted to marry a girl who was like my mother
And Ingrid Bergman was always impossible
And there's maybe a girl now but she's already married
And I don't like men and—
but there's got to be somebody!
Because what if I'm 60 years old and not married,
all alone in a furnished room with pee stains on my underwear
and everybody else is married! All the universe married but me!

Ah, yet well I know that were a woman possible as I am
        possible
then marriage would be possible—
Like SHE in her lonely alien gaud waiting her Egyptian lover
so I wait—bereft of 2,000 years and the bath of life.

The mock-rational and as-if-mild quality of "because" and "kindly" indicate from the outset that the poet will get away with whatever she wants. A challenge to see if one could write something as matter-of-fact, yet as far-out, as this.

712

Because I could not stop for Death—
He kindly stopped for me—
The Carriage held but just Ourselves—
And Immortality.

We slowly drove—He knew no haste
And I had put away
My labor and my leisure too,
For His Civility—

We passed the School, where Children strove
At Recess—in the Ring—
We passed the Fields of Gazing Grain—
We passed the Setting Sun—

Or rather—He passed Us—
The Dews drew quivering and chill—
For only Gossamer, my Gown—
My Tippet—only Tulle—

We paused before a House that seemed
A swelling of the Ground—
The Roof was scarcely visible—
The Cornice—in the Ground—

Since then—'tis Centuries—and yet
Feels shorter than the Day
I first surmised the Horses' Heads
Were toward Eternity—

She makes fun of the great poet and his poem, and of herself,
and of the reader, sustaining the laughter and the profundity
through this extended high-wire walk, with no safety net.

Thoughts About the Person from Porlock

Coleridge received the Person from Porlock
And ever after called him a curse,
Then why did he hurry to let him in?
He could have hid in the house.

It was not right of Coleridge in fact it was wrong
(But often we all do wrong)
As the truth is I think he was already stuck
With Kubla Khan.

He was weeping and wailing: I am finished, finished,
I shall never write another word of it,
When along comes the Person from Porlock
And takes the blame for it.

It was not right, it was wrong,
But often we all do wrong.

May we inquire the name of the Person from Porlock?
Why, Porson, didn't you know?
He lived at the bottom of Porlock Hill
So had a long way to go,

He wasn't much in the social sense
Though his grandmother was a Warlock,

One of the Rutlandshire ones I fancy
And nothing to do with Porlock,

And he lived at the bottom of the hill as I said
And had a cat named Flo,
And had a cat named Flo.

I long for the Person from Porlock
To bring my thoughts to an end,
I am becoming impatient to see him
I think of him as a friend,

Often I look out of the window
Often I run to the gate
I think, He will come this evening,
I think it is rather late.

I am hungry to be interrupted
For ever and ever amen
O Person from Porlock come quickly
And bring my thoughts to an end.

               •

I felicitate the people who have a Person from Porlock
To break up everything and throw it away
Because then there will be nothing to keep them
And they need not stay.

               •

Why do they grumble so much?
He comes like a benison
They should be glad he has not forgotten them
They might have had to go on.

               •

These thoughts are depressing I know. They are depressing,
I wish I was more cheerful, it is more pleasant,
Also it is a duty, we should smile as well as submitting
To the purpose of One Above who is experimenting
With various mixtures of human character which goes best,
All is interesting for him it is exciting, but not for us.
There I go again. Smile, smile, and get some work to do
Then you will be practically unconscious without positively
    having to go.

*Can you write a lyrical, musical poem with a sentence that
might feel in place as part of an instruction manual? (As does
the second sentence of this poem?)*

Fine Work with Pitch and Copper

Now they are resting
in the fleckless light
separately in unison

like the sacks
of sifted stone stacked
regularly by twos

about the flat roof
ready after lunch
to be opened and strewn

The copper in eight
foot strips has been
beaten lengthwise

down the center at right
angles and lies ready
to edge the coping

One still chewing
picks up a copper strip
and runs his eye along it

KENNETH KOCH, "Variations on a Theme
by William Carlos Williams"

One of the greatest parodies ever: a tribute to Williams' imagi-
nation, as well as clear laughter at the egotism, male chauvin-
ism, self-regard, that are fibers of that imagination.

Variations on a Theme by William Carlos Williams

1

I chopped down the house that you had been saving to live in
    next summer.
I am sorry, but it was morning, and I had nothing to do
and its wooden beams were so inviting

2

We laughed at the hollyhocks together
and then I sprayed them with lye.
Forgive me. I simply do not know what I am doing.

3

I gave away the money that you had been saving to live on for
    the next ten years.
The man who asked for it was shabby
and the firm March wind on the porch was so juicy and cold.

4

Last evening we went dancing and I broke your leg.
Forgive me. I was clumsy, and
I wanted you here in the wards, where I am the doctor!

ALAN DUGAN, "How We Heard the Name"

"Ba-bas"! "Whom / all of you ba-bas"! The "whom," the drunk soldier's careful grammar, make him and his superior attitude toward "us" more interesting.

How We Heard the Name

The river brought down
dead horses, dead men
and military debris,
indicative of war
or official acts upstream,
but it went by, it all
goes by, that is the thing
about the river. Then
a soldier on a log
went by. He seemed drunk
and we asked him Why
had he and this junk
come down to us so
from the past upstream.
"Friends," he said, "the great
Battle of Granicus
has just been won
by all of the Greeks except
the Lacedaemonians and
myself: this is a joke
between me and a man
named Alexander, whom
all of you ba-bas
will hear of as a god."

JAMES SHIRLEY, "The Glories of Our Blood and State"

Abstractions. As in many poems by John Ashbery, as though in defiance of a standard creative writing dictum, a masterful series of abstractions. Also, the scythe and spade, the icy hand, the altar, are the equivalent of abstractions, not vivid images. How does this work so well? Or doesn't it? Is this poem the opposite of Dugan's "How We Heard the Name," or similar to it?

The Glories of Our Blood and State

The glories of our blood and state
    Are shadows, not substantial things;
There is no armour against Fate;
    Death lays his icy hand on kings:
        Sceptre and Crown
        Must tumble down,
And in the dust be equal made
With the poor crooked scythe and spade.

Some men with swords may reap the field,
    And plant fresh laurels where they kill:
But their strong nerves at last must yield;
    They tame but one another still:
        Early or late
        They stoop to fate,
And must give up their murmuring breath
When they, pale captives, creep to death.

The garlands wither on your brow;
    Then boast no more your mighty deeds!

Upon Death's purple altar now
    See where the victor-victim bleeds.
        Your heads must come
        To the cold tomb:
Only the actions of the just
Smell sweet and blossom in their dust.

EDWARD THOMAS, "Adlestrop"

Freedom includes the freedom to engage the ordinary, to press into it and find its connection to plenitude or mystery. Write a poem about a name or word.

Adlestrop

Yes. I remember Adlestrop—
The name, because one afternoon
Of heat the express-train drew up there
Unwontedly. It was late June.

The steam hissed. Someone cleared his throat.
No one left and no one came
On the bare platform. What I saw
Was Adlestrop—only the name

And willows, willow-herb, and grass,
And meadowsweet, and haycocks dry,
No whit less still and lonely fair
Than the high cloudlets in the sky.

And for that minute a blackbird sang
Close by, and round him, mistier,
Farther and farther, all the birds
Of Oxfordshire and Gloucestershire.

ANDREW MARVELL, "Upon Appleton House"

The best workplace occasional poem ever written, meandering and full of in-jokes and references, like a wedding toast or the speech someone makes at an office party, family celebration, school event—but with the difference that Marvell makes it great. A model of the wandering, free-floating, yet purposeful long poem. Possibly, best to begin with selections: e.g., the last four stanzas.

Upon Appleton House, to my Lord Fairfax

I.

Within this sober Frame expect
Work of no Forrain *Architect* ;
That unto Caves the Quarries drew,
And Forrests did to Pastures hew ;
Who of his great Design in pain
Did for a Model vault his Brain,
Whose Columnes should so high be rais'd
To arch the Brows that on them gaz'd.

II.

Why should of all things Man unrul'd
Such unproportion'd dwellings build?
The Beasts are by their Denns exprest :
And Birds contrive an equal Nest ;
The low roof'd Tortoises do dwell
In cases fit of Tortoise-shell :
No Creature loves an empty space ;
Their Bodies measure out their Place.

III.

But He, superfluously spread,
Demand more room alive than dead.

And in his hollow Palace goes
Where Winds as he themselves may lose.
What need of all this Marble Crust
T'impark the wanton Mote of Dust,
That thinks by Breadth the World t'unite
Though the first Builders fail'd in Height?

IV.

But all things are composed here
Like Nature, orderly and near :
In which we the Dimensions find
Of that more sober Age and Mind,
When larger sized Men did stoop
To enter at a narrow loop ;
As practising, in doors so strait,
To strain themselves through *Heavens Gate*.

V.

And surely when the after Age
Shall hither come in *Pilgrimage*,
These sacred Places to adore,
By *Vere* and *Fairfax* trod before,
Men will dispute how their Extent
Within such dwarfish Confines went :
And some will smile at this, as well
As *Romulus* his Bee-like Cell.

VI.

Humility alone designs
Those short but admirable Lines,
By which, ungirt and unconstrain'd,
Things greater are in less contain'd.
Let others vainly strive t'immure
The *Circle* in the *Quadrature* !
These *holy Mathematicks* can
In ev'ry Figure equal Man.

VII.

Yet thus the laden House does sweat,
And scarce indures the *Master* great :
But where he comes the swelling Hall
Stirs, and the *Square* grows *Spherical* ;
More by his *Magnitude* distrest,
Than he is by its straitness prest :
And too officiously it slights
That in it self which him delights.

VIII.

So Honour better Lowness bears,
Than That unwonted Greatness wears.
Height with a certain Grace does bend,
But low Things clownishly ascend.
And yet what needs there here Excuse,
Where ev'ry Thing does answer Use ?
Where neatness nothing can condemn,
Nor Pride invent what to contemn ?

IX.

A Stately *Frontispice of Poor*
Adorns without the open Door :
Nor less the Rooms within commends
Daily new *Furniture of Friends.*
The House was built upon the Place
Only as for *a Mark of Grace* ;
And for an *Inn* to entertain
Its *Lord* a while, but not remain.

X.

Him *Bishops-Hill*, or *Denton* may,
Or *Bilbrough*, better hold than they :
But Nature here hath been so free
As if she said leave this to me.

Art would more neatly have defac'd
What she had laid so sweetly wast ;
In fragrant Gardens, shaddy Woods,
Deep Meadows, and transparent Floods.

XI.

While with slow Eyes we these survey,
And on each pleasant footstep stay,
We opportunly may relate
The Progress of this Houses Fate.
A *Nunnery* first gave it birth.
For *Virgin Buildings* oft brought forth.
And all that Neighbour-Ruine shows
The Quarries whence this dwelling rose.

XII.

Near to this gloomy Cloysters Gates
There dwelt the blooming Virgin *Thwates* ;
Fair beyond Measure, and an Heir
Which might Deformity make fair.
And oft She spent the Summer Suns
Discoursing with the *Suttle Nunns.*
Whence in these Words one to her weav'd,
(As 'twere by Chance) Thoughts long conceiv'd.

XIII.

' Within this holy leisure we
' Live innocently as you see.
' These Walls restrain the World without,
' But hedge our Liberty about.
' These Bars inclose that wider Den
' Of those wild Creatures, called Men.
' The Cloyster outward shuts its Gates,
' And, from us, locks on them the Grates.

XIV.

' Here we, in shining Armour white,
' Like *Virgin Amazons* do fight.
' And our chast *Lamps* we hourly trim,
' Lest the great *Bridegroom* find them dim.
' Our *Orient* Breaths perfumed are
' With insense of incessant Pray'r.
' And Holy-water of our Tears
' Most strangly our Complexion clears.

XV.

' Not Tears of Grief ; but such as those
' With which calm Pleasure overflows ;
' Or Pity, when we look on you
' That live without this happy Vow.
' How should we grieve that must be seen
' Each one a *Spouse*, and each a *Queen* ;
' And can in *Heaven* hence behold
' Our brighter Robes and Crowns of Gold ?

XVI.

' When we have prayed all our Beads,
' Some One the holy *Legends* reads ;
' While all the rest with Needles paint
' The Face and Graces of the *Saint*.
' But what the Linnen can't receive
' They in their Lives do interweave.
' This Work the *Saints* best represents ;
' That serves for *Altar's* Ornaments.

XVII.

' But much it to our work would add
' If here your hand, your Face we had :
' By it we would *our Lady* touch ;

' Yet thus She you resembles much,
' Some of your Features, as we sow'd,
' Through ev'ry *Shrine* should be bestow'd.
' And in one Beauty we would take
' Enough a thousand *Saints* to make.

XVIII.

' And (for I dare not quench the Fire
' That me does for your good inspire)
' 'Twere Sacriledge a Man t'admit
' To holy things, for *Heaven* fit.
' I see the *Angels* in a Crown
' On you the Lillies show'ring down :
' And round about you Glory breaks,
' That something more than humane speaks.

XIX.

' All Beauty, when at such a height,
' Is so already consecrate.
' *Fairfax* I know ; and long ere this
' Have mark'd the Youth, and what he is.
' But can he such a *Rival* seem
' For whom you *Heav'n* should disesteem ?
' Ah, no ! and 'twould more Honour prove
' He your *Devoto* were, than *Love*.

XX.

' Here live beloved, and obey'd :
' Each one your Sister, each your Maid.
' And, if our Rule seem strictly pend,
' The Rule it self to you shall bend.
' Our *Abbess* too, now far in Age,
' Doth your succession near presage.
' How soft the yoke on us would lye,
' Might such fair Hands as yours it tye !

XXI.

' Your voice, the sweetest of the Quire,
' Shall draw *Heav'n* nearer, raise us higher.
' And your Example, if our Head,
' Will soon us to perfection lead.
' Those Virtues to us all so dear,
' Will straight grow Sanctity when here :
' And that, once sprung, increase so fast
' Till Miracles it work at last.

XXII.

' Nor is our *Order* yet so nice,
' Delight to banish as a Vice.
' Here Pleasure Piety doth meet ;
' One perfecting the other Sweet.
' So through the mortal fruit we boyl
' The Sugars uncorrupting Oyl :
' And that which perisht while we pull,
' Is thus preserved clear and full.

XXIII.

' For such indeed are all our Arts ;
' Still handling Natures finest Parts.
' Flow'rs dress the Altars ; for the Clothes,
' The Sea-born Amber we compose ;
' Balms for the griv'd we draw ; and Pasts
' We mold, as Baits for curious tasts.
' What need is here of Man ? unless
' These as sweet Sins we should confess.

XXIV.

' Each Night among us to your side
' Appoint a fresh and Virgin Bride ;
' Whom if *our Lord* at midnight find,

' Yet Neither should be left behind.
' Where you may lye as chast in Bed,
' As Pearls together billeted.
' All Night embracing Arm in Arm,
' Like Chrystal pure with Cotton warm.

XXV.

' But what is this to all the store
' Of Joys you see, and may make more !
' Try but a while, if you be wise :
' The Tryal neither Costs, nor Tyes.
Now *Fairfax* seek her promis'd faith :
Religion that dispensed hath ;
Which She hence forward does begin ;
The *Nuns* smooth Tongue has suckt her in.

XXVI.

Oft, though he knew it was in vain,
Yet would he valiantly complain.
' Is this that *Sanctity* so great,
' An Art by which you finly'r cheat ?
' Hypocrite Witches, hence *avant*,
' Who though in prison yet inchant !
' Death only can such Theeves make fast,
' As rob though in the Dungeon cast.

XXVII.

' Were there but, when this House was made,
' One Stone that a just Hand had laid,
' It must have fall'n upon her Head
' Who first Thee from thy Faith misled.
' And yet, how well soever ment,
' With them 'twould soon grow fraudulent :
' For like themselves they alter all,
' And vice infects the very Wall.

XXVIII.

' But sure those Buildings last not long,
' Founded by Folly, kept by Wrong.
' I know what Fruit their Gardens yield,
' When they it think by Night conceal'd.
' Fly from their Vices. 'Tis thy state,
' Not Thee, that they would consecrate.
' Fly from their Ruine. How I fear
' Though guiltless lest thou perish there.

XXIX.

What should he do ? He would respect
Religion, but not Right neglect :
For first Religion taught him Right,
And dazzled not but clear'd his sight.
Sometimes resolv'd his Sword he draws,
But reverenceth then the Laws :
For Justice still that Courage led ;
First from a Judge, then Souldier bred.

XXX.

Small Honour would be in the Storm.
The *Court* him grants the lawful Form ;
Which licens'd either Peace or Force,
To hinder the unjust Divorce.
Yet still the *Nuns* his Right debar'd,
Standing upon their holy Guard.
Ill-counsell'd Women, do you know
Whom you resist, or what you do ?

XXXI.

Is not this he whose Offspring fierce
Shall fight through all the *Universe* ;
And with successive Valour try
France, Poland, either *Germany* ;

Till one, as long since prophecy'd,
His Horse through conquer'd *Britain* ride ?
Yet, against Fate, his Spouse they kept ;
And the great Race would intercept.

XXXII.

Some to the Breach against their Foes
Their *Wooden Saints* in vain oppose.
Another bolder stands at push
With their old *Holy-Water Brush*.
While the disjointed *Abbess* threads
The gingling Chain-shot of her *Beads*.
But their lowd'st Cannon were their Lungs ;
And sharpest Weapons were their Tongues.

XXXIII.

But, waving these aside like Flyes,
Young *Fairfax* through the Wall does rise.
Then th' unfrequented Vault appear'd,
And superstitions vainly fear'd.
The *Relicks false* were set to view ;
Only the Jewels there were true.
But truly bright and holy *Thwaites*
That weeping at the *Altar* waites.

XXXIV.

But the glad Youth away her bears,
And to the *Nuns* bequeaths her Tears :
Who guiltily their Prize bemoan,
Like Gipsies that a Child hath stoln.
Thenceforth (as when th'Inchantment ends
The Castle vanishes or rends)
The wasting Cloister with the rest
Was in one instant dispossest.

XXXV.

At the demolishing, this Seat
To *Fairfax* fell as by Escheat.
And what both *Nuns* and *Founders* will'd
'Tis likely better thus fulfill'd.
For if the *Virgin* prov'd not theirs,
The *Cloyster* yet remained hers.
Though many a *Nun* there made her Vow,
'Twas no *Religious House* till now.

XXXVI.

From that blest Bed the *Heroe* came,
Whom *France* and *Poland* yet does fame :
Who, when retired here to Peace,
His warlike Studies could not cease ;
But laid these Gardens out in sport
In the just Figure of a Fort ;
And with five Bastions it did fence,
As aiming one for ev'ry Sense.

XXXVII.

When in the *East* the Morning Ray
Hangs out the Colours of the Day,
The Bee through these known Allies hums,
Beating the *Dian* with its *Drumms*.
Then Flow'rs their drowsie Eylids raise,
Their Silken Ensigns each displayes,
And dries its Pan yet dank with Dew,
And fills its Flask with Odours new.

XXXVIII.

These, as their *Governour* goes by,
In fragrant Vollyes they let fly ;
And to salute their *Governess*

Again as great a charge they press :
None for the *Virgin Nymph* ; for She
Seems with the Flow'rs a Flow'r to be.
And think so still ! though not compare
With Breath so sweet, or Cheek so faire.

XXXIX.

Well shot ye Firemen ! Oh how sweet,
And round your equal Fires do meet ;
Whose shrill report no Ear can tell,
But Ecchoes to the Eye and smell.
See how the Flow'rs, as at *Parade*,
Under their *Colours* stand displaid :
Each *Regiment* in order grows,
That of the Tulip Pinke and Rose.

XL.

But when the vigilant *Patroul*
Of Stars walks round about the *Pole*,
Their Leaves, that to the stalks are curl'd,
Seem to their Staves the *Ensigns* furl'd.
Then in some Flow'rs beloved Hut
Each Bee as Sentinel is shut ;
And sleeps so too : but, if once stir'd,
She runs you through, or askes *the Word*.

XLI.

Oh Thou, that dear and happy Isle
The Garden of the World ere while,
Thou *Paradise* of four Seas,
Which *Heaven* planted us to please,
But, to exclude the World, did guard
With watry if not flaming Sword ;
What luckless Apple did we tast,
To make us Mortal, and The Wast ?

XLII.

Unhappy ! shall we never more
That sweet *Militia* restore,
When Gardens only had their Towrs,
And all the Garrisons were Flowrs,
When Roses only Arms might bear,
And Men did rosie Garlands wear ?
Tulips, in several Colours barr'd,
Were then the *Switzers* of our *Guard.*

XLIII.

The *Gardiner* had the *Souldiers* place,
And his more gentle Forts did trace.
The Nursery of all things green
Was then the only *Magazeen.*
The *Winter Quarters* were the Stoves,
Where he the tender Plants removes.
But War all this doth overgrow :
We Ord'nance Plant and Powder sow.

XLIV.

And yet their walks one on the Sod
Who, had it pleased him and *God,*
Might once have made our Gardens spring
Fresh as his own and flourishing.
But he preferr'd to the *Cinque Ports*
These five imaginary Forts :
And, in those half-dry Trenches, spann'd
Pow'r which the Ocean might command.

XLV.

For he did, with his utmost Skill,
Ambition weed, but *Conscience* till.
Conscience, that Heaven-nursed Plant,

Which most our Earthly Gardens want.
A prickling leaf it bears, and such
As that which shrinks at ev'ry touch ;
But Flowrs eternal, and divine,
That in the Crowns of Saints do shine.

XLVI.

The sight does from these *Bastions* ply,
Th' invisible *Artilery* ;
And at proud *Cawood Castle* seems
To point the *Battery* of its Beams.
As if it quarrell'd in the Seat
Th' Ambition of its *Prelate* great.
But ore the Meads below it plays,
Or innocently seems to gaze.

XLVII.

And now to the Abbyss I pass
Of that unfathomable Grass,
Where Men like Grashoppers appear,
But Grashoppers are Gyants there :
They, in there squeking Laugh, contemn
Us as we walk more low than them :
And, from the Precipices tall
Of the green spir's, to us do call.

XLVIII.

To see Men through this Meadow Dive,
We wonder how they rise alive.
As, under Water, none does know
Whether he fall through it or go.
But, as the Marriners that sound,
And show upon their Lead the Ground,
They bring up Flow'rs so to be seen,
And prove they've at the Bottom been.

XLIX.

No Scene that turns with Engines strange
Does oftner than these Meadows change.
For when the Sun the Grass hath vext,
The tawny Mowers enter next ;
Who seem like *Israelites* to be,
Walking on foot through a green Sea.
To them the Grassy Deeps divide,
And crowd a Lane to either Side.

L.

With whistling Sithe, and Elbow strong,
These Massacre the Grass along :
While one, unknowing, carves the *Rail*,
Whose yet unfeather'd Quils her fail.
The Edge all bloody from its Breast
He draws, and does his stroke detest ;
Fearing the Flesh untimely mow'd
To him a Fate as black forebode.

LI.

But bloody *Thestylis*, that waites
To bring the mowing Camp their Cates,
Greedy as Kites has trust it up,
And forthwith means on it to sup :
When on another quick She lights,
And cryes, he call'd us *Israelites* ;
But now, to make his saying true,
Rails rain for Quails, for Manna Dew.

LII.

Unhappy birds ! what does it boot
To build below the Grasses Root ;
When Lowness is unsafe as Hight,

And Chance o'retakes what scapeth spight ?
And now your Orphan Parents Call
Sounds your untimely Funeral.
Death-Trumpets creak in such a Note,
And 'tis the *Sourdine* in their Throat.

LIII.

Or sooner hatch or higher build :
The Mower now commands the Field ;
In whose new Traverse seemeth wrought
A Camp of Battail newly fought:
Where, as the Meads with Hay, the Plain
Lyes quilted ore with Bodies slain :
The Women that with forks it fling,
Do represent the Pillaging.

LIV.

And now the careless Victors play,
Dancing the Triumphs of the Hay ;
Where every Mowers wholesome Heat
Smells like an *Alexanders sweat.*
Their Females fragrant as the Mead
Which they in *Fairy Circles* tread :
When at their Dances End they kiss,
Their new-made Hay not sweeter is.

LV.

When after this 'tis pil'd in Cocks,
Like a calm Sea it shews the Rocks :
We wondering in the River near
How Boats among them safely steer.
Or, like the *Desert Memphis Sand*,
Short *Pyramids* of Hay do stand.
And such the *Roman Camps* do rise
In Hills for Soldiers Obsequies.

LVI.

This *Scene* again withdrawing brings
A new and empty Face of things ;
A levell'd space, as smooth and plain,
As Clothes for *Lilly* strecht to stain.
The World when first created sure
Was such a Table rase and pure.
Or rather such is the *Toril*
Ere the Bulls enter at Madril.

LVII.

For to this naked equal Flat,
Which *Levellers* take Pattern at,
The Villagers in common chase
Their Cattle, which it closer rase ;
And what below the Sith increast
Is pincht yet nearer by the Beast.
Such, in the painted World, appear'd
Davenant with th' Universal Heard.

LVIII.

They seem within the polisht Grass
A Landskip drawen in Looking-Glass.
And shrunk in the huge Pasture show
As Spots, so shap'd, on Faces do.
Such Fleas, ere they approach the Eye,
In Multiplying Glasses lye.
They feed so wide, so slowly move,
As *Constellations* do above.

LIX.

Then, to conclude these pleasant Acts,
Denton sets ope its *Cataracts* ;
And makes the Meadow truly be

(What it but seem'd before) a Sea.
For, jealous of its *Lords* long stay,
It try's t'invite him thus away.
The River in it self is drown'd,
And Isl's th' astonish'd Cattle round.

LX.

Let others tell the *Paradox*,
How Eels now bellow in the Ox ;
How Horses at their Tails do kick,
Turn'd as they hang to leeches quick ;
How Boats can over Bridges sail ;
And Fishes do the Stables scale.
How *Salmons* trespassing are found ;
And Pikes are taken in the Pound.

LXI.

But I, retiring from the Flood,
Take Sanctuary in the Wood ;
And, while it lasts, my self imbark
In this yet green, yet growing Ark ;
Where the first Carpenter might best
Fit Timber for his Keel have Prest.
And where all Creatures might have shares,
Although in Armies, not in Paires.

LXII.

The double Wood of ancient Stocks
Link'd in so thick, an Union locks,
It like two *Pedigrees* appears,
On one hand *Fairfax*, th' other *Veres* :
Of whom though many fell in War,
Yet more to Heaven shooting are :
And, as they Natures Cradle deckt,
Will in green Age her Hearse expect.

LXIII.

When first the Eye this Forrest sees
It seems indeed as *Wood* not *Trees* :
As if their Neighbourhood so old
To one great Trunk them all did mold.
There the huge Bulk takes place, as ment
To thrust up a *Fifth Element* ;
And stretches still so closely wedg'd
As if the Night within were hedg'd.

LXIV.

Dark all without it knits ; within
It opens passable and thin ;
And in as loose an order grows,
As the *Corinthean Porticoes.*
The arching Boughs unite between
The Columnes of the Temple green ;
And underneath the winged Quires
Echo about their tuned Fires.

LXV.

The *Nightingale* does here make choice
To sing the Tryals of her Voice.
Low Shrubs she sits in, and adorns
With Musick high the squatted Thorns.
But highest Oakes stoop down to hear,
And listning Elders prick the Ear.
The Thorn, lest it should hurt her, draws
Within the Skin its shrunken claws.

LXVI.

But I have for my Musick found
A Sadder, yet more pleasing Sound :
The *Stock-doves*, whose fair necks are grac'd

With Nuptial Rings their Ensigns chast ;
Yet always, for some Cause unknown,
Sad pair unto the Elms they moan.
O why should such a Couple mourn,
That in so equal Flames do burn !

LXVII.

Then as I carless on the Bed
Of gelid *Straw-berryes* do tread,
And through the Hazles thick espy
The hatching *Thrastles* shining Eye,
The *Heron* from the Ashes top,
The eldest of its young lets drop,
As if it Stork-like did pretend
That *Tribute* to *its Lord* to send.

LXVIII.

But most the *Hewel's* wonders are,
Who here has the *Holt-felsters* care.
He walks still upright from the Root,
Meas'ring the Timber with his Foot ;
And all the way, to keep it clean,
Doth from the Bark the Wood-moths glean.
He, with his Beak, examines well
Which fit to stand and which to fell.

LXIX.

The good he numbers up, and hacks ;
As if he mark'd them with the Ax.
But where he, tinkling with his Beak,
Does find the hollow Oak to speak,
That for his building he designs,
And through the tainted Side he mines.
Who could have thought the *tallest Oak*
Should fall by such a *feeble Strok'* !

LXX.

Nor would it, had the Tree not fed
A *Traitor-worm*, within it bred.
(As first our *Flesh* corrupt within
Tempts impotent and bashful *Sin*.
And yet that *Worm* triumphs not long,
But serves to feed the *Hewels young.*
While the Oake seems to fall content,
Viewing the Treason's Punishment.

LXXI.

Thus I, *easie Philosophe*r,
Among the *Birds* and *Trees* confer :
And little now to make me, wants
Or of the *Fowles*, or of the *Plants.*
Give me but Wings as they, and I
Streight floting on the Air shall fly :
Or turn me but, and you shall see
I was but an inverted Tree.

LXXII.

Already I begin to call
In their most learned Original :
And where I Language want, my Signs
The Bird upon the Bough divines ;
And more attentive there doth sit
Than if She were with Lime-twigs knit.
No Leaf does tremble in the Wind
Which I returning cannot find.

LXXIII.

Out of these scatter'd *Sibyls* Leaves
Strange *Prophecies* my Phancy weaves :
And in one History consumes,

Like *Mexique Paintings*, all the *Plumes*.
What *Rome, Greece, Palestine*, ere said
I in this light *Mosaick* read.
Thrice happy he who, not mistook,
Hath read in *Natures mystick Book*.

   LXXIV.

And see how Chance's better Wit
Could with a Mask my studies hit !
The Oak-Leaves me embroyder all,
Between which Caterpillars crawl :
And Ivy, with familiar trails,
Me licks, and clasps, and curles, and hales.
Under this *antick Cope* I move
Like some great *Prelate of the Grove*,

   LXXV.

Then, languishing with ease, I toss
On Pallets swoln of Velvet Moss ;
While the Wind, cooling through the Boughs,
Flatters with Air my panting Brows.
Thanks for my Rest ye *Mossy Banks*,
And unto you *cool Zephyr's* Thanks,
Who, as my Hair, my Thoughts too shed,
And winnow from the Chaff my Head.

   LXXVI.

How safe, methinks, and strong, behind
These Trees have I incamp'd my Mind ;
Where Beauty, aiming at the Heart,
Bends in some Tree its useless Dart ;
And where the World no certain Shot
Can make, or me it toucheth not.
But I on it securely play,
And gaul its Horsemen all the Day.

LXXVII.

Bind me ye *Woodbines* in your 'twines,
Curle me about ye gadding *Vines*,
And Oh so close your Circles lace,
That I may never leave this Place :
But, lest your Fetters prove too weak,
Ere I your Silken Bondage break,
Do you, *O Brambles*, chain me too,
And courteous *Briars* nail me through.

LXXVIII.

Here in the Morning tye my Chain,
Where the two Woods have made a Lane ;
While, like a *Guard* on either side,
The Trees before their *Lord* divide ;
This, like a long and equal Thread,
Betwixt two *Labyrinths* does lead.
But, where the Floods did lately drown,
There at the Ev'ning stake me down.

LXXIX.

For now the Waves are fal'n and dry'd,
And now the Meadows fresher dy'd ;
Whose Grass, with moister colour dasht,
Seems as green Silks but newly washt.
No *Serpent* new nor *Crocodile*
Remains behind our little *Nile* ;
Unless it self you will mistake,
Among these Meads the only Snake.

LXXX.

See in what wanton harmless folds
It ev'ry where the Meadow holds ;
And its yet muddy back doth lick,

Till as a *Chrystal Mirrour* slick ;
Where all things gaze themselves, and doubt
If they be in it or without.
And for his shade which therein shines,
Narcissus like, the *Sun* too pines.

LXXXI.

Oh what a Pleasure 'tis to hedge
My Temples here with heavy sedge ;
Abandoning my lazy Side,
Stretcht as a Bank unto the Tide ;
Or to suspend my sliding Foot
On the Osiers undermined Root,
And in its Branches tough to hang,
While at my Lines the Fishes twang !

LXXXII.

But now away my Hooks, my Quills,
And Angles, idle Utensils.
The *young Maria* walks to night :
Hide trifling Youth thy Pleasures slight.
'Twere shame that such judicious Eyes
Should with such Toyes a Man surprize ;
She that already is the *Law*
Of all her *Sex*, her *Ages Aw*.

LXXXIII.

See how loose Nature, in respect
To her, it self doth recollect ;
And every thing so whisht and fine,
Starts forth with to its *Bonne Mine*.
The *Sun* himself, of *Her* aware,
Seems to descend with greater Care ;
And lest *She* see him go to Bed ;
In blushing Clouds conceales his Head.

LXXXIV.

So when the Shadows laid asleep
From underneath these Banks do creep,
And on the River as it flows
With *Eben Shuts* begin to close ;
The modest *Halcyon* comes in sight,
Flying betwixt the Day and Night ;
And such an horror calm and dumb,
Admiring Nature does benum.

LXXXV.

The viscous Air, wheres'ere She fly,
Follows and sucks her Azure dy ;
The gellying Stream compacts below,
If it might fix her shadow so ;
The stupid Fishes hang, as plain
As *Flies* in *Chrystal* overt'ane ;
And Men the silent *Scene* assist,
Charm'd with the *Saphir-winged Mist.*

LXXXVI.

Maria such, and so doth hush
The *World*, and through the *Ev'ning* rush.
No new-born *Comet* such a Train
Draws through the Skie, nor Star new-slain.
For straight those giddy Rockets fail,
Which from the putrid Earth exhale,
But by her *Flames*, in *Heaven* try'd,
Nature is wholly *vitrifi'd.*

LXXXVII.

'Tis *She* that to these Gardens gave
That wondrous Beauty which they have ;
She straightness on the Woods bestows ;

To *Her* the Meadow sweetness owes ;
Nothing could make the River be
So Chrystal-pure but only *She* ;
She yet more Pure, Sweet, Streight, and Fair,
Then Gardens, Woods, Meads, Rivers are.

LXXXVIII.

Therefore what first *She* on them spent,
They gratefully again present.
The Meadow Carpets where to tread ;
The Garden Flow'rs to Crown *Her* Head ;
And for a Glass the limpid Brook,
Where *She* may all *her* Beautyes look ;
But, since *She* would not have them seen,
The Wood about *her* draws a Skreen.

LXXXIX.

For *She*, to higher Beauties rais'd,
Disdains to be for lesser prais'd.
She counts her Beauty to converse
In all the Languages as *hers* ;
Nor yet in those *her self* imployes
But for the *Wisdome*, not the *Noyse* ;
Nor yet that *Wisdome* would affect,
But as 'tis *Heavens Dialect.*

LXL.

Blest Nymph ! that couldst so soon prevent
Those *Trains* by Youth against thee meant ;
Tears (watry Shot that pierce the Mind ;)
And *Sighs* (Loves Cannon charg'd with Wind ;)
True Praise (That breaks through all defence ;)
And *feign'd complying Innocence* ;
But knowing where this *Ambush* lay,
She scap'd the safe, but roughest Way.

LXLI.

This 'tis to have been from the first
In a *Domestick Heaven* nurst,
Under the *Discipline* severe
Of *Fairfax*, and the starry *Vere* ;
Where not one object can come nigh
But pure, and spotless as the Eye ;
And *Goodness* doth it self intail
On *Females*, if there want a *Male*.

LXLII.

Go now fond Sex that on your Face
Do all your useless Study place,
Nor once at Vice your Brows dare knit
Lest the smooth Forehead wrinkled sit :
Yet your own Face shall at you grin,
Thorough the Black-bag of your Skin ;
When *knowledge* only could have fill'd
And *Virtue* all those *Furrows till'd*.

LXLIII.

Hence *She* with Graces more divine
Supplies beyond her *Sex* the *Line* ;
And, like a *sprig of Misleto*,
On the *Fairfacian Oak* does grow ;
Whence, for some universal good,
The *Priest* shall cut the sacred Bud ;
While her *glad Parents* most rejoice,
And make their *Destiny* their *Choice*.

LXLIV.

Mean time ye Fields, Springs, Bushes, Flow'rs,
Where yet She leads her studious Hours,
(Till Fate her worthily translates,

And find a *Fairfax* for our *Thwaites*)
Employ the means you have by Her,
And in your kind your selves prefer ;
That, as all *Virgins* She preceds,
So you all *Woods, Streams, Gardens, Meads*.

LXLV.

For you *Thessalian Tempe's Seat*
Shall now be scorn'd as obsolete ;
Aranjuez, as less, disdain'd ;
The *Bel-Retiro* as constrain'd ;
But name not the *Idalian Grove*,
For 'twas the Seat of wanton Love ;
Much less the Dead's *Elysian Fields*,
Yet nor to them your Beauty yields.

LXLVI.

'Tis not, what once it was, the *World* ;
But a rude heap together hurl'd ;
All negligently overthrown,
Gulfes, Deserts, Precipices, Stone.
Your lesser *World* contains the same.
But in more decent Order tame ;
You Heaven's Center, Nature's Lap.
And Paradice's only Map.

LXLVII.

But now the *Salmon-Fishers* moist
Their *Leathern Boats* begin to hoist ;
And, like *Antipodes* in Shoes,
Have shod their *Heads* in their *Canoos.*
How *Tortoise like*, but not so slow,
These rational *Amphibii* go ?
Let 's in : for the dark *Hemisphere*
Does now like one of them appear.

JONATHAN SWIFT, "A Description of the Morning"

Try your own, contemporary version of this, in your own
world, keeping it fresh yet recognizable—good luck.

A Description of the Morning

Now hardly here and there an Hackney-Coach
Appearing, show'd the Ruddy Morns Approach.
Now *Betty* from her Masters Bed had flown,
And softly stole to discompose her own.
The Slipshod Prentice from his Masters Door,
Had par'd the Dirt, and Sprinkled round the Floor.
Now *Moll* had whirl'd her Mop with dext'rous Airs,
Prepar'd to Scrub the Entry and the Stairs.
The Youth with Broomy Stumps began to trace
The Kennel-Edge, where Wheels had worn the Place.
The Smallcoal-Man was heard with Cadence deep,
'Till drown'd in Shriller Notes of Chimney-Sweep,
Duns at his Lordships Gate began to meet,
And Brickdust *Moll* had Scream'd through half the Street.
The Turnkey now his Flock returning sees,
Duly let out a-Nights to Steal for Fees.
The watchful Bailiffs take their silent Stands,
And School-Boys lag with Satchels in their Hands.

Sexy, as well as nasty, poem about erectile dysfunction/premature ejaculation. She had her nerve, and the good sense not to show off about it.

The Disappointment

One day the amorous Lysander,
By an impatient passion swayed,
Surprised fair Cloris, that loved maid,
Who could defend her self no longer.
All things did with his love conspire;
The gilded planet of the day,
In his gay chariot drawn by fire,
Was now descending to the sea,
And left no light to guide the world,
But what from Cloris brighter eyes was hurled.

In a lone thicket made for love,
Silent as yielding maids consent,
She with a charming languishment,
Permits his force, yet gently strove;
Her hands his bosom softly meet,
But not to put him back designed,
Rather to draw 'em on inclined:
Whilst he lay trembling at her feet,
Resistance 'tis in vain to show;
She wants the power to say—*Ah! What d'ye do?*

Her bright eyes sweet, and yet severe,
Where love and shame confus'dly strive,
Fresh vigour to Lysander give;
And breathing faintly in his ear,

She cried—*Cease, cease—your vain desire,*
Or I'll call out—What would you do?
My dearer honour ev'n to you
I cannot, must not give—Retire,
Or take this life, whose chiefest part
I gave you with the conquest of my heart.

But he as much unused to fear,
As he was capable of love,
The blessed minutes to improve,
Kisses her mouth, her neck, her hair;
Each touch her new desire alarms,
His burning trembling hand he pressed
Upon her swelling snowy breast,
While she lay panting in his arms.
All her unguarded beauties lie
The spoils and trophies of the enemy.

And now without respect or fear,
He seeks the object of his vows,
(His love no modesty allows)
By swift degrees advancing—where
His daring hand that altar seized,
Where gods of love do sacrifice:
That awful throne, that paradise
Where rage is calmed and anger pleased;
That fountain where delight still flows,
And gives the universal world repose.

Her balmy lips encount'ring his,
Their bodies, as their souls, are joined;
Where both in transports unconfined
Extend themselves upon the moss.
Cloris half dead and breathless lay;
Her soft eyes cast a humid light,

Such as divides the day and night;
Or falling stars, whose fires decay:
And now no signs of life she shows,
But what in short-breathed sighs returns and goes.

He saw how at her length she lay;
He saw her rising bosom bare;
Her loose thin robes, through which appear
A shape designed for love and play;
Abandoned by her pride and shame.
She does her softest joys dispense,
Off'ring her virgin-innocence
A victim to love's sacred flame;
While the o'er-ravished shepherd lies
Unable to perform the sacrifice.

Ready to taste a thousand joys,
The too transported hapless swain
Found the vast pleasure turned to pain;
Pleasure which too much love destroys:
The willing garments by he laid,
And heaven all opened to his view,
Mad to possess, himself he threw
On the defenceless lovely maid.
But Oh what envying god conspires
To snatch his power, yet leave him the desire!

Nature's support, (without whose aid
She can no human being give)
Itself now wants the art to live;
Faintness its slackened nerves invade:
In vain th' enraged youth essayed
To call its fleeting vigour back,
No motion 'twill from motion take;
Excess of love his love betrayed:

In vain he toils, in vain commands;
The Insensible fell weeping in his hand.

In this so amorous cruel strife,
Where love and fate were too severe,
The poor Lysander in despair
Renounced his reason with his life:
Now all the brisk and active fire
That should the nobler part inflame,
Served to increase his rage and shame,
And left no spark for new desire:
Not all her naked charms could move
Or calm that rage that had debauched his love.

Cloris returning from the trance
Which love and soft desire had bred,
Her timorous hand she gently laid
(Or guided by design or chance)
Upon that fabulous Priapus,
That potent god, as poets feign;
But never did young shepherdess,
Gath'ring of fern upon the plain,
More nimbly draw her fingers back,
Finding beneath the verdant leaves a snake:

Than Cloris her fair hand withdrew,
Finding that god of her desires
Disarmed of all his awful fires,
And cold as flow'rs bathed in the morning dew.
Who can the Nymph's confusion guess?
The blood forsook the hinder place,
And strewed with blushes all her face,
Which both disdain and shame expressed:
And from Lysander's arms she fled,
Leaving him fainting on the gloomy bed.

Like lightning through the grove she hies,
Or Daphne from the Delphic God,
No print upon the grassy road
She leaves, t' instruct pursuing eyes.
The wind that wantoned in her hair,
And with her ruffled garments played,
Discovered in the flying maid
All that the gods e'er made, if fair.
So Venus, when her Love was slain,
With fear and haste flew o'er the fatal plain.

The Nymph's resentments none but I
Can well imagine or condole:
But none can guess Lysander's soul,
But those who swayed his destiny.
His silent griefs swell up to storms,
And not one god his fury spares;
He cursed his birth, his fate, his stars;
But more the shepherdess's charms,
Whose soft bewitching influence
Had damned him to the Hell of impotence.

The shook foil, the crushed oil, the brown sky: images of the then-incipient Industrial Revolution: a fresh, innovative bit of attention that he does not linger on, because he has a larger purpose: freedom to see anew, enabled by that driving purpose. Freedom comes from purpose.

God's Grandeur

The world is charged with the grandeur of God.
    It will flame out, like shining from shook foil;
    It gathers to a greatness, like the ooze of oil
Crushed. Why do men then now not reck his rod?
Generations have trod, have trod, have trod;
    And all is seared with trade; bleared, smeared with toil;
    And wears man's smudge and shares man's smell: the soil
Is bare now, nor can foot feel, being shod.

And, for all this, nature is never spent;
    There lives the dearest freshness deep down things;
And though the last lights off the black West went
    Oh, morning, at the brown brink eastward, springs—
Because the Holy Ghost over the bent
    World broods with warm breast and with ah! bright wings.

Unashamed to be performative, preening, hyper-rational.
Unashamed of the national stereotypes and other elements of
clowning. It's worth pondering how he manages to keep it
changing and progressing, rather than settling into a predict-
able groove. The answer to that question is related to how he
gives it urgency, seriousness, agile thought—in a word,
meaning.

Upon Nothing

Nothing! thou elder brother even to Shade:
Thou hadst a being ere the world was made,
And well fixed, art alone of ending not afraid.

Ere Time and Place were, Time and Place were not,
When primitive Nothing Something straight begot;
Then all proceeded from the great united What.

Something, the general attribute of all,
Severed from thee, its sole original,
Into thy boundless self must undistinguished fall;

Yet Something did thy mighty power command,
And from thy fruitful Emptiness's hand
Snatched men, beasts, birds, fire, water, air, and land.

Matter, the wicked'st offspring of thy race,
By Form assisted, flew from thy embrace,
And rebel Light obscured thy reverend dusky face.

With Form and Matter, Time and Place did join;
Body, thy foe, with these did leagues combine
To spoil thy peaceful realm, and ruin all thy line;

But turncoat Time assists the foe in vain,
And bribed by thee, destroys their short-lived reign,
And to thy hungry womb drives back thy slaves again.

Though mysteries are barred from laic eyes,
And the divine alone with warrant pries
Into thy bosom, where the truth in private lies,

Yet this of thee the wise may truly say:
Thou from the virtuous nothing dost delay,
And to be part of thee the wicked wisely pray.

Great Negative, how vainly would the wise
Inquire, define, distinguish, teach, devise,
Didst thou not stand to point their blind philosophies!

Is or Is Not, the two great ends of Fate,
And True or False, the subject of debate,
That perfect or destroy the vast designs of state—

When they have racked the politician's breast,
Within thy bosom most securely rest,
And when reduced to thee, are least unsafe and best.

But Nothing, why does Something still permit
That sacred monarchs should in council sit
With persons highly thought at best for nothing fit,

While weighty Something modestly abstains
From princes' coffers, and from statesmen's brains,
And Nothing there like stately Nothing reigns?

Nothing! who dwellst with fools in grave disguise,
For whom they reverend shapes and forms devise,
Lawn sleeves and furs and gowns, when they like thee
    look wise:

French truth, Dutch prowess, British policy,
Hibernian learning, Scotch civility,
Spaniards' dispatch, Danes' wit are mainly seen in thee;

The great man's gratitude to his best friend,
Kings' promises, whores' vows—towards thee they bend,
Flow swiftly into thee, and in thee ever end.

II

LISTENING

MUSICIANS DEALING WITH a new or difficult piece may speak of "getting it under your fingers." Athletes, meaning something similar, refer to "body knowledge." The art of poetry has its equivalents. One of them is getting by heart some lines you admire. To memorize (for example) Robert Frost's "To Earthward" (p. 98) or Marianne Moore's "Silence" (p. 15) is to learn something about the bodily nature of poetry.

A certain kind of knowledge comes from following the dance between sentences and lines as they coincide or pull against one another, in a shifting multitude of ways and degrees. And that dance is related to the simultaneous movement of the grammar and line coursing through the harmonic structure of consonants and vowels. The voice recognizes all of that movement and pause, similarity and difference: recognizes it and understands it, in a mental and physical process that could be called, adapting the musician's phrase, "getting it into your voice." The energy of the poem becomes more clear as you assimilate it into your memory, feeling it in your voice.

I'll take as an example the two-line poem by Landor that begins this section (p. 82). Some readers will memorize it without trying:

> On love, on grief, on every human thing,
> Time sprinkles Lethe's water with his wing.

The great cliché that time flies and the ancient cultural furniture of Lethe, the river of forgetting in Hades, are transformed here partly by imagination: wings propel, but they also sprinkle, and forgetting too may be sprinkled and incremental, rather than a tidal wave.

But those ideas do not fully explain the freshness and immediacy I feel every time I say Landor's poem. An essential part of the poem is physical. Three times, at the beginning, I put my upper teeth on my lower lip, to create the consonants in the words "love," grief," and "every." And three times, at the end, I purse my lips to create the consonants in the words "water," "with," and "wing."

Noting those triads doesn't begin to exhaust all that's going on in the vocal sounds of this fifteen-word poem. It is good to learn about iambs and pentameters, but the art of such a poem is inexhaustible beyond any prosody or notation.

Was Landor thinking about those three fricative sounds at the beginning of his poem and the three *w* sounds at the end? I doubt it very much—no more than an athlete or musician thinks about each mechanical aspect of a moment that takes about as much time as saying this poem. Athletes and musicians practice, and consider small matters of mechanics, precisely so that they do not need to think about them in performance. Like an actor who memorizes lines perfectly, the artist can concentrate on the performance, the feeling, confident that the means, acquired over time by hard work, will be in place.

This is a matter of technique more than interpretation, at a level and kind of technical detail quite different from literary criticism. In the course of memorizing just the first few lines of Emily Dickinson's "The Soul Selects Her Own Society," (p. 105), one gets a new, corporeal appreciation of the like vowel sound in "soul" and "own," with the like consonant sound of "selects" and "shuts," echoed in "notes the Chariots." And those vowels and consonants return in the poem's final word, "Stone." Rhyme is the least of it, or just one obvious aspect of it.

In my experience, noticing such things does not diminish one's pleasure in the poem by "picking it apart." On the contrary, fine-grained, technical understanding can heighten pleasure. The person who understands more about any kind of excellence, with access to a fine, wide range of detail, has more to enjoy. At the ballet, the dog show, the boxing match, the opera, the museum, someone who knows more than I do has a wider access to the pleasures of what is there. The fluid pleasure in the whole can avail itself of detail or not, in the freedom of choice.

Dizzy Gillespie was not only a pioneer among jazz musicians, an innovative genius as improvising performer and composer; he was also known as a great teacher of his peers. Accomplished, eminent musicians wanted to learn from him: "Piano players, bass players, saxophone players," as he says in his Fall 1965 *Paris Review* interview, "They call me, and come over to my house to work."

In that interview, Gillespie makes remarks that apply profoundly to writing poetry. The bebop innovator, the master of intricate, experimental harmony, says:

About the harmony—some guys really ran some of our ideas into the ground. A lot of times something just isn't suitable, you know? They didn't use it with any taste. I think the *basic* part of jazz is rhythm and you should delve into that. But, you see, the trouble is that a lot of guys can't keep time. I mean that they can't see two or three rhythms going at once, so all they can do is mess with the chords.

Interviewer: Could you clarify the statement that what is most important in jazz is rhythm? Some people think jazz is rhythmically simple, or primitive. All they hear is the steady beat and nothing else.

Gillespie: "I'm not talking about that! Rhythmic content means how you *accent*, where your accents are, and how they fit in with different types of rhythm. You can't notate it for them; they have to be able to hear it. You can come close, but you can't really write jazz.

In poetry, too, followers may run the ideas that impress them into the ground. In poetry, too, originality may depend on taste. In poetry, too, the scaffold or egg crate of scansion is not the same as rhythm. The actual, vocal rhythm is more subtle than any notation on the page. The typography indicates the vocal rhythm or hints at it. Hearing the thousands of possibilities, so that even "you can't really write jazz" has an application to the poet's art: strictly speaking, you don't write a poem, you compose it.

A bit further in the interview, Gillespie says about choosing among thousands of rhythmic possibilities in a split second, and playing one: "It isn't instinct. It's hard!" That is, you need to study. Composing a poem with real rhythm, choosing phrases for cadence and melody while feeling the flux of emotions and ideas, resembles that split-second process of the improvising musician. Here are two examples, one from so-called "metrical" verse and one from "free" verse. First (p. 96):

AN OLD MAN'S WINTER NIGHT

All out-of-doors looked darkly in at him
Through the thin frost, almost in separate stars,
That gathers on the pane in empty rooms.
What kept his eyes from giving back the gaze
Was the lamp tilted near them in his hand.
What kept him from remembering what it was
That brought him to that creaking room was age.
He stood with barrels round him—at a loss.
And having scared the cellar under him
In clomping here, he scared it once again
In clomping off;—and scared the outer night,
Which has its sounds, familiar, like the roar

Of trees and crack of branches, common things,
But nothing so like beating on a box.
A light he was to no one but himself
Where now he sat, concerned with he knew what,
A quiet light, and then not even that.
He consigned to the moon, such as she was,
So late-arising, to the broken moon
As better than the sun in any case
For such a charge, his snow upon the roof,
His icicles along the wall to keep;
And slept. The log that shifted with a jolt
Once in the stove disturbed him, and he shifted,
And eased his heavy breathing, but still slept.
One aged man—one man—can't keep a house,
A farm, a countryside, or if he can,
It's thus he does it of a winter night.

The poem is in iambic pentameter, and it can be scanned, but that is a bit like saying a tune is in 4/4 time; the information is helpful but minimal. In the first eight or nine lines, Gillespie's remarks about accents, distinct from a metronomic beat, apply to the way "gaze," "eyes," "was," and "stars" share a consonant sound while "gaze," "pane," and "age" share a vowel sound.

Hearing such things, let alone using them in the work of original composition, demands practice: a kind of study far beyond the child's play of scansion or memorized terminology. Sometimes in the course of tasteful, inventive expression, a sentence or part of a sentence may fit the verse line exactly:

He stood with barrels round him—at a loss.
But nothing so like beating on a box.

Sometimes, the sentence stretches over and across the metrical line:

Which has its sounds, familiar, like the roar
Of trees and crack of branches, common things

                  The log that shifted with a jolt
Once in the stove disturbed him, and he shifted.

To point out such matters, as I've tried to do, is not more than a
signpost. To actually learn from them requires studying them in
one's particular way, like an instrumentalist playing a piece over
and studying how it is put together.

    The second example (p. 29):

FINE WORK WITH PITCH AND COPPER

Now they are resting
in the fleckless light
separately in unison

like the sacks
of sifted stone stacked
regularly by twos

about the flat roof
ready after lunch
to be opened and strewn

The copper in eight
foot strips has been
beaten lengthwise

down the center at right
angles and lies ready
to edge the coping

One still chewing
picks up a copper strip
and runs his eye along it

Here, too, the energy comes partly from a formal interlacing of vowels and consonants: the short *e* sound in "resting," "fleck-less," "separately," and "regularly" with consonants that recur in the "sifted stone stacked." The vowel of "unison," "twos," "roof," "strewn" succeeds the short *e* a little bit like a change of key. And in the last stanza, "One still chewing / picks up a copper strip" is like a reprise of these sounds.

Does this analysis make things up, or spin imaginary patterns that don't really exist? There is only one way to judge, and if I am right, to learn: that is, by listening.

*The bodily, intimate nature of poetry demonstrated in two
lines: three times, at the beginning, you put your upper teeth on
your lower lip. Three times, at the end, you purse your lips. A
lesson in how to refresh a cliché ("time flies") and in listening.*

On Love, on Grief

On love, on grief, on every human thing,
Time sprinkles Lethe's water with his wing.

The pause as one of the most expressive sounds. The pause—
that crucial bit of silence—is essential to the poetic art of
writing in audible (not merely typographical) lines—and
sometimes it is within the line, not necessarily at the end of it.

Betsabe's Song

Hot sun, cool fire, tempered with sweet air,
Black shade, fair nurse, shadow my white hair:
Shine, sun ; burn, fire ; breathe, air, and ease me;
Black shade, fair nurse, shroud me, and please me:
Shadow, my sweet nurse, keep me from burning,
Make not my glad cause cause of [my] mourning.
            Let not my beauty's fire
            Inflame unstaid desire,
            Nor pierce any bright eye
            That wandereth lightly.

H.D., "The Pool"

More notable than the like sounds echoing in "cover," "quiver," and "alive" is how the poet separates or counters the richness, keeps it from being too sugary.

The Pool

Are you alive?
I touch you.
You quiver like a sea-fish.
I cover you with my net.
What are you—banded one?

The ballad raised, as in algebra, to the ballad power: a hyper-
ballad. Dazzling rhyme. An interesting exercise might be to
find or create an equivalent poem in free verse, without much
end rhyme. H.D.'s poems, maybe?

Eros Turannos

She fears him, and will always ask
   What fated her to choose him;
She meets in his engaging mask
   All reasons to refuse him;
But what she meets and what she fears
Are less than are the downward years,
Drawn slowly to the foamless weirs
   Of age, were she to lose him.

Between a blurred sagacity
   That once had power to sound him,
And Love, that will not let him be
   The Judas that she found him,
Her pride assuages her almost,
As if it were alone the cost.—
He sees that he will not be lost,
   And waits and looks around him.

A sense of ocean and old trees.
   Envelops and allures him;
Tradition, touching all he sees,
   Beguiles and reassures him;
And all her doubts of what he says
Are dimmed with what she knows of days—
Till even prejudice delays
   And fades, and she secures him.

The falling leaf inaugurates
   The reign of her confusion;
The pounding wave reverberates
   The dirge of her illusion;
And home, where passion lived and died,
Becomes a place where she can hide,
While all the town and harbor side
   Vibrate with her seclusion.

We tell you, tapping on our brows,
   The story as it should be,—
As if the story of a house
   Were told, or ever could be;
We'll have no kindly veil between
Her visions and those we have seen,—
As if we guessed what hers have been,
   Or what they are or would be.

Meanwhile we do no harm; for they
   That with a god have striven,
Not hearing much of what we say,
   Take what the god has given;
Though like waves breaking it may be,
Or like a changed familiar tree,
Or like a stairway to the sea
   Where down the blind are driven.

BEN JONSON, "His Excuse for Loving"

The last sentence, its extended melody, like a great long phrase in music. The flowing, natural speech extended into a sinuous, nuanced melody . . . and under it, the meter of "Twinkle, Twinkle, Little Star."

His Excuse for Loving

Let it not your wonder move,
Less your laughter ; that I love.
Though I now write fifty years,
I have had, and have my peers ;
Poets, though divine, are men :
Some have loved as old again.
And it is not always face,
Clothes, or fortune gives the grace ;
Or the feature, or the youth:
But the language, and the truth,
With the ardour, and the passion,
Gives the lover weight and fashion.
If you then will read the story,
First prepare you to be sorry,
That you never knew till now,
Either whom to love, or how :
But be glad, as soon with me,
When you know, that this is she,
Of whose beauty it was sung,
She shall make the old man young,
Keep the middle age at stay,
And let nothing high decay,
Till she be the reason why,
All the world for love may die.

*In effect, Jonson's lesson in what a line is. And his lines are far
from equal in length, which is instructive.*

My Picture Left in Scotland

I now think, Love is rather deaf, than blind,
  For else it could not be,
    That she,
Whom I adore so much, should so slight me,
  And cast my love behind :
I'm sure my language to her, was as sweet,
    And every close did meet
   In sentence, of as subtle feet,
    As hath the youngest he,
  That sits in shadow of Apollo's tree.

Oh, but my conscious fears,
    That fly my thoughts between,
   Tell me that she hath seen
   My hundreds of grey hairs,
   Told seven and forty years,
  Read so much waist, as she cannot embrace
  My mountain belly, and my rocky face,
And all these through her eyes, have stopped her ears.

*Jonson's friend and follower: they wrote melodies when they
wrote sentences. Compare these couplets to those in Yeats's
"Adam's Curse" (p. 103). Two experts, centuries apart, fitting
sentences to lines in similar ways.*

Upon M. Ben. Johnson

After the rare Arch-Poet JOHNSON dy'd,
The Sock grew loathsome, and the Buskins pride,
Together with the stage's glory stood
Each like a poor and pitied widowhood.
The Cirque prophan'd was; and all postures rackt:
For men did strut, and stride, and stare, not act.
Then temper flew from words; and men did squeak,
Looke red, and blow, and bluster, but not speak:
No Holy-Rage, or frantick-fires did stirr,
Or flash about the spacious Theater.
No clap of hands, or shout, or praises-proof
Did crack the Play-house sides, or cleave her roof.
Artlesse the Scene was; and that monstrous sin
Of deep and *arrant ignorance* came in;
Such ignorance as theirs was, who once hist
At thy unequal'd Play, the *Alchymist*:
Oh fie upon 'em! Lastly too, all wit
In utter darkenes did, and still will sit
Sleeping the luckless Age out, till that she
Her Resurrection has again with Thee.

GERARD MANLEY HOPKINS, "For Margaret"

Hopkins had read Campion, Herrick, Jonson, Shakespeare—
and he made his unique, transforming, original music that
grows out of theirs.

Spring and Fall:

FOR MARGARET

to a Young Child

Margaret, are you grieving
Over Goldengrove unleaving?
Leaves, like the things of man, you
With your fresh thoughts care for, can you?
Ah! as the heart grows older
It will come to such sights colder
By and by, nor spare a sigh
Though worlds of wanwood leafmeal lie;
And yet you *will* weep and know why.
Now no matter, child, the name:
Sorrow's springs are the same.
Nor mouth had, no nor mind, expressed
What héart héard of, ghóst guéssed:
It is the blight man was born for,
It is Margaret you mourn for.

THOMAS CAMPION, "Now Winter Nights Enlarge"

*Study the energy of "enlarge" and "discharge," the energy of
the rhyming verbs at the ends of lines. "Enlarge" as one reads a
contract just means "increase" the number of hours. But as one
reads a poem, it makes the towers and the night larger. Could
one emulate the relation of long lines to short lines?*

Now Winter Nights Enlarge

Now winter nights enlarge
    The number of their hours;
And clouds their storms discharge
    Upon the airy towers.
Let now the chimneys blaze
    And cups o'erflow with wine,
Let well-tuned words amaze
    With harmony divine.
Now yellow waxen lights
    Shall wait on honey love
While youthful revels, masques, and courtly sights
    Sleep's leaden spells remove.

This time doth well dispense
    With lovers' long discourse;
Much speech hath some defense,
    Though beauty no remorse.
All do not all things well;
    Some measures comely tread,
Some knotted riddles tell,
    Some poems smoothly read.
The summer hath his joys,
    And winter his delights;
Though love and all his pleasures are but toys,
    They shorten tedious nights.

THOM GUNN, "Tamer and Hawk"

When you read this aloud, you must keep the sentence-move-
ment pressing ahead, or it dies. The poem shows you that with
the dancing intersections of line and sentence, for example:
"when I go I go / At your commands."

Tamer and Hawk

I thought I was so tough,
But gentled at your hands,
Cannot be quick enough
To fly for you and show
That when I go I go
At your commands.

Even in flight above
I am no longer free:
You seeled me with your love,
I am blind to other birds—
The habit of your words
Has hooded me.

As formerly, I wheel
I hover and I twist,
But only want the feel,
In my possessive thought,
Of catcher and of caught
Upon your wrist.

You but half civilize,
Taming me in this way.
Through having only eyes
For you I fear to lose,
I lose to keep, and choose
Tamer as prey.

*A feminist, modernist, and completely lyrical love complaint—
the desire and impatience with desire both expressed in the
sounds.*

---

from Songs to Joannes

    I

Spawn   of   Fantasies
Silting the appraisable
Pig Cupid   his rosy snout
Rooting erotic garbage
"Once upon a time"
Pulls a weed   white and star-topped
Among wild oats   sewn in mucous-membrane

I would   an   eye in a Bengal light
Eternity in a sky-rocket
Constellations in an ocean

Whose rivers run no fresher
Than a trickle of saliva

These   are suspect places

I must live in my lantern
Trimming subliminal flicker
Virginal   to the bellows
Of Experience
               Coloured   glass

II

                    The skin-sack
In which a wanton duality
Packed
All the completion of my infructuous impulses
Something the shape of a man
To the casual vulgarity of the merely observant
More of a clock-work mechanism
Running down against time
To which I am not paced.
      My finger-tips are numb from fretting your hair
A God's door-mat
                    On the threshold of your mind

III

We might have coupled
In the bed-ridden monopoly of a moment
Or broken flesh with one another
At the profane communion table
Where wine is spill't on promiscuous lips

We might have given birth to a butterfly
With the daily-news
Printed in blood on its wings

> *To my ear, the equivalent of rhyme. "Trees/glaze" is a kind of rhyme, but the like sounds are even richer in (for example) "the snow / is covered with broken / seedhusks": the like vowels of "snow"/"broken" and "covered"/"seedhusks" braided with the like consonants of "is covered"/"seedhusks."*

To Waken an Old Lady

Old age is
a flight of small
cheeping birds
skimming
bare trees
above a snow glaze.
Gaining and failing
they are buffeted
by a dark wind—
But what?
On harsh weedstalks
the flock has rested,
the snow
is covered with broken
seedhusks
and the wind tempered
by a shrill
piping of plenty.

ROBERT FROST, "An Old Man's Winter Night"

Someone who likes exercises and assignments might take this poem as a model: write a poem in five-foot, unrhymed lines, with this kind of sentence.

An Old Man's Winter Night

All out-of-doors looked darkly in at him
Through the thin frost, almost in separate stars,
That gathers on the pane in empty rooms.
What kept his eyes from giving back the gaze
Was the lamp tilted near them in his hand.
What kept him from remembering what it was
That brought him to that creaking room was age.
He stood with barrels round him—at a loss.
And having scared the cellar under him
In clomping here, he scared it once again
In clomping off;—and scared the outer night,
Which has its sounds, familiar, like the roar
Of trees and crack of branches, common things,
But nothing so like beating on a box.
A light he was to no one but himself
Where now he sat, concerned with he knew what,
A quiet light, and then not even that.
He consigned to the moon, such as she was,
So late-arising, to the broken moon
As better than the sun in any case
For such a charge, his snow upon the roof,
His icicles along the wall to keep;
And slept. The log that shifted with a jolt
Once in the stove, disturbed him and he shifted,

And eased his heavy breathing, but still slept.
One aged man—one man—can't keep a house,
A farm, a countryside, or if he can,
It's thus he does it of a winter night.

ROBERT FROST, "To Earthward"

*Read the sentences aloud as sentences, and the rhymes take
care of themselves. Frost is a sexier, more adventuresome poet
than he may get credit for. And in the stanza about being stung
by the petal of the rose, is he laughing at his own exquisite
nature?*

To Earthward

Love at the lips was touch
As sweet as I could bear;
And once that seemed too much;
I lived on air

That crossed me from sweet things,
The flow of—was it musk
From hidden grapevine springs
Down hill at dusk?

I had the swirl and ache
From sprays of honeysuckle
That when they're gathered shake
Dew on the knuckle.

I craved strong sweets, but those
Seemed strong when I was young;
The petal of the rose
It was that stung.

Now no joy but lacks salt
That is not dashed with pain
And weariness and fault;
I crave the stain

Of tears, the aftermark
Of almost too much love,
The sweet of bitter bark
And burning clove.

When stiff and sore and scarred
I take away my hand
From leaning on it hard
In grass and sand,

The hurt is not enough:
I long for weight and strength
To feel the earth as rough
To all my length.

The attentive student of poetry can identify at least three distinct technical ways that the movement in the first half of the poem is different from that in the second half. Not impressions or feelings: objective differences in verse technique.

Nature, That Washed Her Hands in Milk

Nature, that washed her hands in milk
And had forgot to dry them,
Instead of earth took snow and silk
At Love's request, to try them
If she a mistress could compose
To please Love's fancy out of those.

Her eyes he would should be of light,
A violet breath, and lips of jelly,
Her hair not black nor over-bright,
And of the softest down her belly:
As for her inside, he'd have it
Only of wantonness and wit.

At Love's entreaty, such a one
Nature made, but with her beauty
She hath framed a heart of stone,
So as Love, by ill destiny,
Must die for her whom Nature gave him,
Because her darling would not save him.

But Time, which Nature doth despise,
And rudely gives her love the lie,
Makes hope a fool and sorrow wise,
His hands doth neither wash nor dry,

But, being made of steel and rust,
Turns snow and silk and milk to dust.

The light, the belly, lips and breath,
He dims, discolors, and destroys,
With those he feeds (but fills not) Death
Which sometimes were the food of Joys:
Yea, Time doth dull each lively wit,
And dries all wantonness with it.

O cruel Time, which takes in trust
Our youth, our joys, and all we have,
And pays us but with age and dust;
Who in the dark and silent grave,
When we have wandered all our ways,
Shuts up the story of our days.

WALLACE STEVENS, "The House Was Quiet and
the World Was Calm"

*Iambic pentameter, idiomatic and hypnotic. To be plain is
demanding. Compare Stevens' metrical verse in this poem
(iambic pentameters) with his free verse in "Madame La Fleu-
rie" (p. 167). To my ear, they are quite similar: both are idiom-
atic and hypnotic. Same musician, different pieces.*

The House Was Quiet and the World Was Calm

The house was quiet and the world was calm.
The reader became the book; and summer night

Was like the conscious being of the book.
The house was quiet and the world was calm.

The words were spoken as if there was no book,
Except that the reader leaned above the page,

Wanted to lean, wanted much most to be
The scholar to whom his book is true, to whom

The summer night is like a perfection of thought.
The house was quiet because it had to be.

The quiet was part of the meaning, part of the mind:
The access of perfection to the page.

And the world was calm. The truth in a calm world,
In which there is no other meaning, itself

Is calm, itself is summer and night, itself
Is the reader leaning late and reading there.

An account of a conversation—and in rhymed couplets. The form feels natural, the speech convincing, partly because of the enjambments and some light rhymes ("poetry"/"maybe," "clergymen"/"thereupon," "school"/"beautiful," "enough"/"love," "strove"/"love," "grown"/"moon"). A masterly example of verse writing, as well as a great poem.

Adam's Curse

We sat together at one summer's end,
That beautiful mild woman, your close friend,
And you and I, and talked of poetry.
I said, "A line will take us hours maybe;
Yet if it does not seem a moment's thought,
Our stitching and unstitching has been naught.
Better go down upon your marrow-bones
And scrub a kitchen pavement, or break stones
Like an old pauper, in all kinds of weather;
For to articulate sweet sounds together
Is to work harder than all these, and yet
Be thought an idler by the noisy set
Of bankers, schoolmasters, and clergymen
The martyrs call the world."

                And thereupon
That beautiful mild woman for whose sake
There's many a one shall find out all heartache
On finding that her voice is sweet and low
Replied, "To be born woman is to know—
Although they do not talk of it at school—
That we must labour to be beautiful."

I said, "It's certain there is no fine thing
Since Adam's fall but needs much labouring.
There have been lovers who thought love should be
So much compounded of high courtesy
That they would sigh and quote with learned looks
Precedents out of beautiful old books;
Yet now it seems an idle trade enough."

We sat grown quiet at the name of love;
We saw the last embers of daylight die,
And in the trembling blue-green of the sky
A moon, worn as if it had been a shell
Washed by time's waters as they rose and fell
About the stars and broke in days and years.

I had a thought for no one's but your ears:
That you were beautiful, and that I strove
To love you in the old high way of love;
That it had all seemed happy, and yet we'd grown
As weary-hearted as that hollow moon.

EMILY DICKINSON, "The Soul Selects Her Own Society"

Get it by heart.

303

The Soul selects her own Society—
Then—shuts the Door—
To her divine Majority—
Present no more—

Unmoved—she notes the Chariots—pausing—
At her low Gate—
Unmoved—an Emperor be kneeling
Upon her Mat—

I've known her—from an ample nation—
Choose One—
Then—close the Valves of her attention—
Like Stone—

III

FORM

ERE'S ANOTHER WAY of thinking about "body knowledge" and poetry. Pursuing excellence, athletes and musicians willingly, even eagerly, submit themselves to tedious, grinding repetition and analysis. They try to cultivate by practice the most effective way of doing each thing, each best movement so reliably summoned that you don't need to think about it in the fluid, immediate, rapid, intuitive performance of your skills. The goal, in a word used by those who work in these pursuits: to perfect their form.

But beyond that process, or extending it, true form is creative. As a verb, "form" means to make or generate. (In a neat parallel, the verb "generate" is related to the noun "genre.") Coaches rightly speak of the best form, but there is no mechanical template: true form is what each person discovers, enhancing or adapting it each time. Form is what makes the batted ball sail over the fence, or the leaping dancer sail across the stage, and for no two people is the successful form exactly alike. Similarities may be important, and they are worth studying, but the best form has an element of idiosyncrasy. Everyone is different. And in practice, any one person will hit the ball or leap a bit differently each time.

In keeping with that flexibility, form should be transformative and original. It can elevate the ordinary, re-sharpen the familiar:

You that seek what life is in death
Now find it air that once was breath:
New names unknown, old names gone,
Till time end bodies, but souls none.
    Reader! then make time, while you be,
    But steps to your eternity.

The author of this poem (p. 133), Fulke Greville, a sixteenth-
century Christian, did not invent the idea that in trying to com-
prehend death one confronts an absence. Nor did Greville invent
the idea that life is short, or that life is followed by eternity. Such
conventional, unoriginal notions do not generate a poem, nor
does religious doctrine, nor does even an emotion—not even a
strong emotion of mingled urgency and dread.

Thinking about breath and air does, perhaps, begin to gener-
ate a poem, because considering those two forms of air, particu-
lar and general, inward and outward, mortal and eternal, may
help create the form of a poem.

Greville's poem involves unstable or unequal pairs of nouns,
beginning (and in a way ending) with *life* and *death*. Air and
breath, new names and old names, bodies and souls, in four lines
arranged in rhymed couplets. In the fourth line, the additional or
unpaired noun "time" complicates the symmetry. Except for the
first, the lines divide symmetrically, with a central pause between
nearly equal halves. That pattern of even twos is broken by the
final, clinching couplet. There, the first of those two final lines is
divided by an emphatic, dramatic pause that comes asymmetri-
cally early in the line, not in the middle: "Reader!" The final line
too is divided asymmetrically, with a less emphatic but distinct
pause after "steps."

"Reader!"—the moment marking that small but effective
deviation in the pattern of pauses—might be called a formal
intrusion or swerve: from declaration to address. And the sen-
tence that follows has three nouns rather than two, with the

opposed duo "time" (no longer unpaired) and "eternity" separated by the intervening "steps."

To describe the form, as I've just tried to do, has required more words than the poem itself: a disproportion between act and description familiar to anyone who has tried to describe even a few moments in a movie, dance, or sporting event, where elements that are familiar are deployed in a way that astounds. In ways that go beyond what can be described, form enables emotion, in shapes of speed and suspension. Form concentrates force.

No recipe predetermines Greville's poem. Its form does not arise from some construction like: *"A form consisting of three iambic tetrameter couplets, with asymmetrical pauses in the first and last two lines, with the final couplet serving as an indented conclusion or critique or turn."* On the contrary, that recipe is an after-the-fact reduction. The poem discovers a form that is beyond description or reduction. It is a unique play of symmetry and asymmetry, energy and balance.

The poetic line is a means of performing energy and balance in writing. As in other kinds of performance, or in editing a movie, the relation between pause and movement is essential to writing in lines. From the same period as Greville's poem, consider George Peele's "Betsabe's Song" (p. 83):

> Hot sun, cool fire, tempered with sweet air,
> Black shade, fair nurse, shadow my white hair:
> Shine, sun; burn, fire; breathe, air, and ease me;
> Black shade, fair nurse, shroud me and please me:
> Shadow, my sweet nurse, keep me from burning,
> Make not my glad cause cause of [my] mourning.
>> Let not my beauty's fire
>> Inflame unstaid desire,
>> Nor pierce any bright eye
>> That wandereth lightly.

Silence is part of rhythm: a truism these pauses demonstrate. But the pauses are made effective by the varying kinds of change and movement around them. In each of the first two lines, a pair of two-syllable, adjective-noun units ("hot sun" and "cool fire," then "black shade" and "fair nurse") are followed by the longer units ("tempered with sweet air," then "shadow my white hair"). The remarkable third line, with its imperative verbs, makes a pause after every syllable, until "and ease me" feels relatively long in contrast, balancing the tension, though it is only three syllables.

In other words, the poem has the taste, which could also be called efficiency or purpose, to keep the rhythm changing and moving. Emotion comes partly from the intense balance of hesitation with explosive force. The line "Inflame unstaid desire" compresses these energies into three words: verb, adjective, noun, all three with the same rhythm: "ta-*da*."

To say George Peele's poem aloud (as one should) is to hear something essential about the nature of lines and the nature of form. The early modernist H.D., in free-verse lines, creates a similar force, partly from pauses and the varying lengths of the units around the pauses (p. 126):

SEA ROSE

Rose, harsh rose,
marred and with stint of petals,
meager flower, thin,
sparse of leaf,

more precious
than a wet rose
single on a stem—
you are caught in the drift.

Stunted, with small leaf,
you are flung on the sand,
you are lifted

in the crisp sand
that drives in the wind.

Can the spice-rose
drip such acrid fragrance
hardened in a leaf?

H.D.'s harsh, sparse, and acrid rose represents a certain sense of beauty, and of poetry. Her defense of something beleaguered, "stunted," "caught in the drift," with its rhythms of halting and pressing forward, has some formal similarity (along with plenty of difference) to George Peele's words for the threatened, vulnerable Bathsheba.

It's possible to think of both Peele and H.D. creating these examples like someone noodling at a piano, toying with chords, or someone pushing paint around on a surface, toying with forms and colors. Of course a poem may originate from ideas, feelings, plans, but a kind of line can be generative in a physical way. One could study the art of poetry, trying to enhance one's sense of form, by thinking about kinds of line. There are countless variables, among them the length of the lines, uniform or varying, the degree and timing of enjambment, iambic or loose iambic or not iambic at all, arranged in stanzas or not, degree and kind of rhyme, end rhyme or not, degree and kind of intensity on a range from prose to incantation, etc. Possibly more useful than such categories, here are some examples:

Elizabeth Bishop syncopating a straightforward, reason-bound narrative, in even four-beat lines, by subtly countering the line with grammatical units that flow across the lines, often end-stopped, but in a self-correcting, parenthetical or not-quite-even way that makes the narrative a bit weirder, less straightforward, in "The Weed" (p. 154):

A few drops fell upon my face
and in my eyes, so I could see

(or, in that black space, thought I saw)
that each drop contained a light,
a small, illuminated scene;
the weed-deflected stream was made
itself of racing images.

Ben Jonson stretching sentences across lines of very different lengths, crazily varying, in "My Picture Left in Scotland" (p. 88):

I now think, Love is rather deaf, than blind,
For else it could not be,
      That she,
Whom I adore so much, should so slight me,
   And cast my love behind:
I'm sure my language to her, was as sweet,
    And every close did meet
    In sentence, of as subtle feet,
    As hath the youngest he,
That sits in shadow of Apollo's tree.

Robert Frost, in "To Earthward" (p. 98), separating iambic pentameter's three-foot and two-foot units and arranging them into a four-line stanza of three, three, three, two, which creates overlapping pentameters at the borders of each stanza. So, for instance, "I lived on air" serves as the second part of one pentameter (*And once that seemed too much; I lived on air*) and the first part of another (*I lived on air / That crossed me from sweet things*):

Love at the lips was touch
As sweet as I could bear;
And once that seemed too much;
I lived on air

That crossed me from sweet things,
The flow of—was it musk

Wallace Stevens deploying repetitions to launch an incantational, long line, in "Madame La Fleurie" (p. 167):

> Weight him, weight, weight him with the sleepiness of the
> moon.

Alan Dugan tossing one outrageous end rhyme—a moment of drinking song or limerick, transforming the lines around it—into a poem otherwise without end rhyme, amending or disrupting the rapid, short, free-verse line in "How We Heard the Name" (p. 31):

> but it went by, it all
> goes by, that is the thing
> about the river. Then
> a soldier on a log
> went by. He seemed drunk
> and we asked him Why
> had he and this junk
> come down to us so
> from the past upstream.

Creating a writing assignment for oneself by trying to make a poem with a formal element, with a deployment of lines somehow like these (or unlike them, in reaction!) is demanding, in a good sense of the word. Finding a form, or a kind of line, can be instructive precisely because it is difficult—yet possible. Following the formula for a sonnet or sestina, with certain patterns at the ends of lines, also may be instructive; but sometimes the formula can become merely a way of evading the nature of the line. Writing that conforms to the recipe for "a form" may or may not have the quality of form. At worst, "forms" can be a poor substitute (or excuse?) for actual form.

Putting aside the idea of models or formulas, what's the best process, in the pursuit of form? The answer will be different for different writers at different moments. But one suggestion might be to say or at least mutter some words—words you think, or have read, or have heard spoken—and keep listening, patiently and calmly, for something that feels right in their arrangement.

ANONYMOUS, "The Cruel Mother"

The refrain a little more cruel each time. "Rarely" = "eagerly,"
a meaning surviving in a rare steak, taken eagerly from the fire.
Like the leaves, the infant is eager to live, and so is the woman.
So few words, many of them (such as "babe") repeated. With
the refrain, the total number of different words is small, yet the
story is told with tremendous force and clarity. Refrain is
mighty, and repetition is basic.

The Cruel Mother

She sat down below a thorn,
   Fine flowers in the valley;
And there she has her sweet babe born,
   And the green leaves they grow rarely.

"Smile na sae sweet, my bonnie babe,"
   Fine flowers in the valley,
"And ye smile sae sweet, ye'll smile me dead,"
   And the green leaves they grow rarely.

She's taen out her little penknife,
   Fine flowers in the valley,
And twinn'd the sweet babe o' its life,
   And the green leaves they grow rarely.

She's howket a grave by the light o' the moon,
   Fine flowers in the valley,
And there she's buried her sweet babe in,
   And the green leaves they grow rarely.

As she was going to the church,
   Fine flowers in the valley,

She saw a sweet babe in the porch,
   And the green leaves they grow rarely.

"O sweet babe, and thou were mine,"
   Fine flowers in the valley,
"I wad cleed thee in the silk so fine,"
   And the green leaves they grow rarely.

"O mother dear, when I was thine,
   Fine flowers in the valley,
Ye did na prove to me sae kind,"
   And the green leaves they grow rarely.

ANONYMOUS, "The Man of Double Deed"

The power of a formula. Beyond explanation. Could you write a sinister or mysterious nursery rhyme? If someone convinced you that this poem was a political allegory, might it diminish your pleasure in the poem? Maybe enhance it? Or, most likely, not affect your enjoyment much one way or the other?

The Man of Double Deed

There was a man of double deed,
Who sowed his garden full of seed;
When the seed began to grow,
'Twas like a garden full of snow;
When the snow began to melt,
'Twas like a ship without a belt;
When the ship began to sail,
'Twas like a bird without a tail;
When the bird began to fly,
'Twas like an eagle in the sky;
When the sky began to roar,
'Twas like a lion at my door;
When my door began to crack,
'Twas like a stick across my back;
When my back began to smart,
'Twas like a penknife in my heart;
And when my heart began to bleed,
'Twas death, and death, and death indeed.

CHIDIOCK TICHBORNE, "My Prime of Youth Is but a Frost of Cares"

Said to have been composed by Tichborne the night before his execution. The relentlessness of the formula and the relentlessness of his fate. If we allow "fall'n," the poem is written entirely in words of one syllable. Could you do that?

My Prime of Youth Is but a Frost of Cares

My prime of youth is but a frost of cares,
My feast of joy is but a dish of pain,
My crop of corn is but a field of tares,
And all my good is but vain hope of gain;
The day is past, and yet I saw no sun,
And now I live, and now my life is done.

My tale was heard and yet it was not told,
My fruit is fallen and yet my leaves are green,
My youth is spent and yet I am not old,
I saw the world and yet I was not seen;
My thread is cut and yet it is not spun,
And now I live, and now my life is done.

I sought my death and found it in my womb,
I looked for life and saw it was a shade,
I trod the earth and knew it was my tomb,
And now I die, and now I was but made;
My glass is full, and now my glass is run,
And now I live, and now my life is done.

SAPPHO, "Artfully Adorned Aphrodite"
(translated by Jim Powell)

*"Whom this time?" "Who now?"—laughter at herself, across
all those centuries and in an ancient language. She makes the
joke on herself, but the joke does not deny the truth of her pas-
sionate arousal. The songlike repetitions and parallelisms, the
formality-mixed-with-passion: a model of love poetry, at the
category's early dawn.*

Artfully Adorned Aphrodite

Artfully adorned Aphrodite, deathless
child of Zeus and weaver of wiles I beg you
please don't hurt me, don't overcome my spirit,
        goddess, with longing,

but come here, if ever at other moments
hearing these my words from afar you listened
and responded: leaving your father's house, all
        golden, you came then,

hitching up your chariot: lovely sparrows
drew you quickly over the dark earth, whirling
on fine beating wings from the heights of heaven
        down through the sky and

instantly arrived—and then O my blessed
goddess with a smile on your deathless face you
asked me what the matter was *this* time, what I
        called you for this time,

what I now most wanted to happen in my
raving heart: "Whom *this* time should I persuade to

lead you back again to her love? Who *now*, oh
    Sappho, who wrongs you?

If she flees you now, she will soon pursue you;
if she won't accept what you give, she'll give it;
if she doesn't love you, she'll love you soon now,
    even unwilling."

Come to me again, and release me from this
want past bearing. All that my heart desires to
happen—make it happen. And stand beside me,
    goddess, my ally.

WILLIAM CARLOS WILLIAMS, "To a Poor Old Woman"

"They taste good to her." The stanza form analyzes that sentence by using lines to present it three ways, emphasizing how remarkable it is that the viewer can see the affect of the woman eating the plums. You can see her feeling the good taste of them! We take the intricate perception and its four elements for granted, and we take the sentence for granted, until the rhythm of the poem, the lines slicing and amplifying the sentence like a hand gesture or a dance step, makes us notice.

To a Poor Old Woman

munching a plum on
the street a paper bag
of them in her hand

They taste good to her
They taste good
to her. They taste
good to her

You can see it by
the way she gives herself
to the one half
sucked out in her hand

Comforted
a solace of ripe plums
seeming to fill the air
They taste good to her

THOMAS NASHE, "In Time of Plague"

In the mostly abandoned streets of plague-time, amid smolder-
ing fires, people were paid to chant the refrain, which sets up a
counter-rhythm to the iambic rhythms of the stanzas. Two
rhythms at once.

In Time of Plague

Adieu, farewell, earth's bliss;
This world uncertain is;
Fond are life's lustful joys;
Death proves them all but toys;
None from his darts can fly;
I am sick, I must die.
    Lord, have mercy on us!

Rich men, trust not in wealth,
Gold cannot buy you health;
Physic himself must fade.
All things to end are made,
The plague full swift goes by;
I am sick, I must die.
    Lord, have mercy on us!

Beauty is but a flower
Which wrinkles will devour;
Brightness falls from the air;
Queens have died young and fair;
Dust hath closed Helen's eye.
I am sick, I must die.
    Lord, have mercy on us!

Strength stoops unto the grave,
Worms feed on Hector brave;
Swords may not fight with fate,
Earth still holds ope her gate.
"Come, come!" the bells do cry.
I am sick, I must die.
    Lord, have mercy on us.

Wit with his wantonness
Tasteth death's bitterness;
Hell's executioner
Hath no ears for to hear
What vain art can reply.
I am sick, I must die.
    Lord, have mercy on us.

Haste, therefore, each degree,
To welcome destiny;
Heaven is our heritage,
Earth but a player's stage;
Mount we unto the sky.
I am sick, I must die.
    Lord, have mercy on us.

H.D., "Sea Rose"

Repeated, varying patterns of stress that avoid prose on one side and iambs on the other. For instance, in the fifth and six lines, the adjoining stressed syllables "more pre-" at the beginning of the two-line unit, echoed at the end by the adjoining stressed syllables "wet rose."

Sea Rose

Rose, harsh rose,
marred and with stint of petals,
meager flower, thin,
sparse of leaf,

more precious
than a wet rose
single on a stem—
you are caught in the drift.

Stunted, with small leaf,
you are flung on the sand,
you are lifted
in the crisp sand
that drives in the wind.

Can the spice-rose
drip such acrid fragrance
hardened in a leaf?

WILLIAM BLAKE, "A Question Answered"

Almost the same thing twice. The "almost" is crucial.

A Question Answered

What is it men in women do require?
The lineaments of Gratified Desire.
What is it women do in men require?
The lineaments of Gratified Desire.

See the anaphora (like beginnings) in Ginsberg's "Howl." Try it and transform it.

---

from Jubilate Agno

For I will consider my Cat Jeoffry.

For he is the servant of the Living God, duly and daily serving him.

For at the first glance of the glory of God in the East he worships in his way.

For is this done by wreathing his body seven times round with elegant quickness.

For then he leaps up to catch the musk, which is the blessing of God upon his prayer.

For he rolls upon prank to work it in.

For having done duty and received blessing he begins to consider himself.

For this he performs in ten degrees.

For first he looks upon his forepaws to see if they are clean.

For secondly he kicks up behind to clear away there.

For thirdly he works it upon stretch with the forepaws extended.

For fourthly he sharpens his paws by wood.

For fifthly he washes himself.

For sixthly he rolls upon wash.

For seventhly he fleas himself, that he may not be interrupted upon the beat.

For eighthly he rubs himself against a post.

For ninthly he looks up for his instructions.

For tenthly he goes in quest of food.

For having considered God and himself he will consider his
    neighbor.
For if he meets another cat he will kiss her in kindness.
For when he takes his prey he plays with it to give it a chance.
For one mouse in seven escapes by his dallying.
For when his day's work is done his business more properly
    begins.
For he keeps the Lord's watch in the night against the
    adversary.
For he counteracts the powers of darkness by his electrical skin
    and glaring eyes.
For he counteracts the Devil, who is death, by brisking about
    the life.
For in his morning orisons he loves the sun and the sun loves
    him.
For he is of the tribe of Tiger.
For the Cherub Cat is a term of the Angel Tiger.
For he has the subtlety and hissing of a serpent, which in
    goodness he suppresses.
For he will not do destruction if he is well-fed, neither will he
    spit without provocation.
For he purrs in thankfulness when God tells him he's a good
    Cat.
For he is an instrument for the children to learn benevolence
    upon.
For every house is incomplete without him, and a blessing is
    lacking in the spirit.
For the Lord commanded Moses concerning the cats at the
    departure of the Children of Israel from Egypt.
For every family had one cat at least in the bag.
For the English Cats are the best in Europe.
For he is the cleanest in the use of his forepaws of any
    quadruped.
For the dexterity of his defense is an instance of the love of God
    to him exceedingly.

For he is the quickest to his mark of any creature.

For he is tenacious of his point.

For he is a mixture of gravity and waggery.

For he knows that God is his Saviour.

For there is nothing sweeter than his peace when at rest.

For there is nothing brisker than his life when in motion.

For he is of the Lord's poor, and so indeed is he called by
benevolence perpetually—Poor Jeoffry! poor Jeoffry! the rat
has bit thy throat.

For I bless the name of the Lord Jesus that Jeoffry is better.

For the divine spirit comes about his body to sustain it in
complete cat.

For his tongue is exceeding pure so that it has in purity what it
wants in music.

For he is docile and can learn certain things.

For he can sit up with gravity, which is patience upon
approbation.

For he can fetch and carry, which is patience in employment.

For he can jump over a stick, which is patience upon proof
positive.

For he can spraggle upon waggle at the word of command.

For he can jump from an eminence into his master's bosom.

For he can catch the cork and toss it again.

For he is hated by the hypocrite and miser.

For the former is afraid of detection.

For the latter refuses the charge.

For he camels his back to bear the first notion of business.

For he is good to think on, if a man would express himself
neatly.

For he made a great figure in Egypt for his signal services.

For he killed the Icneumon rat, very pernicious by land.

For his ears are so acute that they sting again.

For from this proceeds the passing quickness of his attention.

For by stroking of him I have found out electricity.

For I perceived God's light about him both wax and fire.

For the electrical fire is the spiritual substance which God sends
    from heaven to sustain the bodies both of man and beast.
For God has blessed him in the variety of his movements.
For, though he cannot fly, he is an excellent clamberer.
For his motions upon the face of the earth are more than any
    other quadruped.
For he can tread to all the measures upon the music.
For he can swim for life.
For he can creep.

Simple means, familiar sentiments, only forty-one words, no
metaphors—but it has power. Why? Form gives it conviction.

You That Seek What Life Is in Death

You that seek what life is in death,
Now find it air that once was breath.
New names unknown, old names gone:
Till time end bodies, but souls none.
      Reader! then make time, while you be,
      But steps to your eternity.

I dare you to read this poem aloud without being moved by it—and without learning something about poetry from it. The form was called "Poulter's Measure": six feet in one line, seven in the next. Guess what that has to do with selling chickens and eggs.

Elegy for Philip Sidney

Silence augmenteth grief, writing increaseth rage,
Staled are my thoughts, which loved and lost the wonder of
    our age;
Yet quickened now with fire, though dead with frost ere now,
Enraged I write I know not what; dead, quick, I know not how.

Hard-hearted minds relent and rigor's tears abound,
And envy strangely rues his end, in whom no fault was found.
Knowledge her light hath lost, valor hath slain her knight,
Sidney is dead, dead is my friend, dead is the world's delight.

Place, pensive, wails his fall whose presence was her pride ;
Time crieth out, My ebb is come; his life was my spring tide.
Fame mourns in that she lost the ground of her reports ;
Each living wight laments his lack, and all in sundry sorts.

He was (woe worth that word!) to each well-thinking mind
A spotless friend, a matchless man, whose virtue ever shined ;
Declaring in his thoughts, his life, and that he writ,
Highest conceits, longest foresights, and deepest works of wit.

He, only like himself, was second unto none,
Whose death (though life) we rue, and wrong, and all in vain
    do moan ;

Their loss, not him, wail they that fill the world with cries,
Death slew not him, but he made death his ladder to the skies.

Now sink of sorrow I who live—the more the wrong!
Who wishing death, whom death denies, whose thread is all
    too long;
Who tied to wretched life, who looks for no relief,
Must spend my ever dying days in never ending grief.

Farewell to you, my hopes, my wonted waking dreams,
Farewell, sometimes enjoyëd joy, eclipsëd are thy beams.
Farewell, self-pleasing thoughts which quietness brings forth,
And farewell, friendship's sacred league, uniting minds of
    worth.

And farewell, merry heart, the gift of guiltless minds,
And all sports which for life's restore variety assigns;
Let all that sweet is, void; in me no mirth may dwell:
Philip, the cause of all this woe, my life's content, farewell!

Now rhyme, the son of rage, which art no kin to skill,
And endless grief, which deads my life, yet knows not how to
    kill,
Go, seek that hapless tomb, which if ye hap to find
Salute the stones that keep the limbs that held so good a mind.

See the anaphora in Christopher Smart's "Jubilate Agno."
Does anaphora always create a sense of litany, even ritual?
Could you write something where it has a very different feeling
from either of these examples?

from Howl

II

What sphinx of cement and aluminum bashed open their skulls
 and ate up their brains and imagination?
Moloch! Solitude! Filth! Ugliness! Ashcans and unobtainable
 dollars! Children screaming under the stairways! Boys
 sobbing in armies! Old men weeping in the parks!
Moloch! Moloch! Nightmare of Moloch! Moloch the loveless!
 Mental Moloch! Moloch the heavy judger of men!
Moloch the incomprehensible prison! Moloch the crossbone
 soulless jailhouse and Congress of sorrows! Moloch whose
 buildings are judgment! Moloch the vast stone of war!
 Moloch the stunned governments!
Moloch whose mind is pure machinery! Moloch whose blood is
 running money! Moloch whose fingers are ten armies!
 Moloch whose breast is a cannibal dynamo! Moloch whose
 ear is a smoking tomb!
Moloch whose eyes are a thousand blind windows! Moloch
 whose skyscrapers stand in the long streets like endless
 Jehovahs! Moloch whose factories dream and croak in the
 fog! Moloch whose smokestacks and antennae crown the
 cities!
Moloch whose love is endless oil and stone! Moloch whose soul
 is electricity and banks! Moloch whose poverty is the

specter of genius! Moloch whose fate is a cloud of sexless
hydrogen! Moloch whose name is the Mind!

Moloch in whom I sit lonely! Moloch in whom I dream Angels!
Crazy in Moloch! Cocksucker in Moloch! Lacklove and
manless in Moloch!

Moloch who entered my soul early! Moloch in whom I am a
consciousness without a body! Moloch who frightened me
out of my natural ecstasy! Moloch whom I abandon! Wake
up in Moloch! Light streaming out of the sky!

Moloch! Moloch! Robot apartments! invisible suburbs! skeleton
treasuries! blind capitals! demonic industries! spectral
nations! invincible madhouses! granite cocks! monstrous
bombs!

They broke their backs lifting Moloch to Heaven! Pavements,
trees, radios, tons! lifting the city to Heaven which exists
and is everywhere about us!

Visions! omens! hallucinations! miracles! ecstasies! gone down
the American river!

Dreams! adorations! illuminations! religions! the whole
boatload of sensitive bullshit!

Breakthroughs! over the river! flips and crucifixions! gone
down the flood! Highs! Epiphanies! Despairs! Ten years'
animal screams and suicides! Minds! New loves! Mad
generation! down on the rocks of Time!

Real holy laughter in the river! They saw it all! the wild eyes!
the holy yells! They bade farewell! They jumped off the
roof! to solitude! waving! carrying flowers! Down to the
river! into the street!

*Recurrence, not refrain—but with a refrain-like force and
authority. The multiple figures of speech (the horse, the hound),
with each one implying that any one is inadequate: another
kind of repetition.*

Question

Body my house
my horse my hound
what will I do
when you are fallen

Where will I sleep
How will I ride
What will I hunt

Where can I go
without my mount
all eager and quick
How will I know
in thicket ahead
is danger or treasure
when Body my good
bright dog is dead

How will it be
to lie in the sky
without roof or door
and wind for an eye

With cloud for shift
how will I hide?

The repeated "I" takes on a monumental, historical dimension while still feeling personal.

The Negro Speaks of Rivers

I've known rivers:
I've known rivers ancient as the world and older than the flow
    of human blood in human veins.

My soul has grown deep like the rivers.

I bathed in the Euphrates when dawns were young.
I built my hut near the Congo and it lulled me to sleep.
I looked upon the Nile and raised the pyramids above it.
I heard the singing of the Mississippi when Abe Lincoln went
    down to New Orleans, and I've seen its muddy bosom turn
    all golden in the sunset.

I've known rivers:
Ancient, dusky rivers.

My soul has grown deep like the rivers.

GEORGE GASCOIGNE, "The Lullaby of a Lover"

The "loving boy" stanza provides an interesting, sixteenth-century example of a man addressing his own "wares." Something worth emulating in how he makes his penis just one part among many?

The Lullaby of a Lover

Sing lullaby, as women do,
Wherewith they bring their babes to rest,
And lullaby can I sing too
As womanly as can the best.
With lullaby they still the child,
And if I be not much beguiled,
Full many wanton babes have I
Which must be stilled with lullaby.

First lullaby my youthful years;
It is now time to go to bed,
For crooked age and hoary hairs
Have won the haven within my head.
With lullaby, then, youth be still;
With lullaby content thy will;
Since courage quails and comes behind,
Go sleep, and so beguile thy mind.

Next, lullaby my gazing eyes,
Which wonted were to glance apace.
For every glass may now suffice
To show the furrows in my face;
With lullaby then wink awhile,
With lullaby your looks beguile;
Let no fair face nor beauty bright
Entice you eft with vain delight.

And lullaby, my wanton will;
Let reason's rule now reign thy thought,
Since all too late I find by skill
How dear I have thy fancies bought;
With lullaby now take thine ease,
With lullaby thy doubts appease.
For trust to this: if thou be still,
My body shall obey thy will.

Eke lullaby, my loving boy,
My little Robin, take thy rest;
Since age is cold and nothing coy,
Keep close thy coin, for so is best;
With lullaby be thou content,
With lullaby thy lusts relent,
Let others pay which hath mo pence;
Thou art too poor for such expense.

Thus lullaby, my youth, mine eyes,
My will, my ware, and all that was.
I can no mo delays devise,
But welcome pain, let pleasure pass;
With lullaby now take your leave,
With lullaby your dreams deceive;
And when you rise with waking eye,
Remember then this lullaby.

Study the grammar. Which is the main verb of the first sentence? Near the end, in "which also shall / Be crumbled," what noun (or nouns?) does "which" refer to?

Church Monuments

While that my soul repairs to her devotion,
Here I intomb my flesh, that it betimes
May take acquaintance of this heap of dust ;
To which the blast of death's incessant motion,
Fed with the exhalation of our crimes,
Drives all at last. Therefore I gladly trust

My body to this school, that it may learn
To spell his elements, and find his birth
Written in dusty heraldry and lines ;
Which dissolution sure doth best discern,
Comparing dust with dust, and earth with earth.
These laugh at jet, and marble put for signs,

To sever the good fellowship of dust,
And spoil the meeting. What shall point out them,
When they shall bow, and kneel, and fall down flat
To kiss those heaps, which now they have in trust?
Dear flesh, while I do pray, learn here thy stem
And true descent: that when thou shalt grow fat,

And wanton in thy cravings, thou mayst know,
That flesh is but the glass, which holds the dust
That measures all our time; which also shall
Be crumbled into dust. Mark, here below,
How tame these ashes are, how free from lust,
That thou mayst fit thyself against thy fall.

The refrain knit into the stanzas. More fun to make your own version of such a thing, maybe, than set forms like sonnet and sestina? Like George Herbert, Hardy tends to make up a form every time he writes a poem.

During Wind and Rain

> They sing their dearest songs—
> He, she, all of them—yea,
> Treble and tenor and bass,
>   And one to play;
> With the candles mooning each face. . . .
>   Ah, no; the years O!
> How the sick leaves reel down in throngs!
>
> They clear the creeping moss—
> Elders and juniors—aye,
> Making the pathways neat
>   And the garden gay;
> And they build a shady seat. . . .
>   Ah, no; the years, the years;
> See, the white storm-birds wing across.
>
> They are blithely breakfasting all—
> Men and maidens—yea,
> Under the summer tree,
>   With a glimpse of the bay,
> While pet fowl come to the knee. . . .
>   Ah, no; the years O!
> And the rotten rose is ript from the wall.

They change to a high new house,
He, she, all of them—aye,
Clocks and carpets and chairs
    On the lawn all day,
And brightest things that are theirs. . . .
    Ah, no; the years, the years
Down their carved names the rain-drop ploughs.

IV

DREAMING
THINGS UP

N A FUNDAMENTAL way, the poet is someone who has something special to say. That is, people in general have timeworn, customary words we utter when we are moved: angry or giddy, grieving or flirting, rejoicing or lamenting. The poet is a particular kind of expert.

On a communal level, if the tribe's search for food has been successful or if the hunt has been unlucky, if someone has been born or died or is getting married, if there has been a military victory or defeat—on such occasions, there are things people say. More personal occasions, such as courtship or elegy, also by human custom come with some expectation of words. As an anthropologist might observe, the words have a conventional, even ritual status. Verbal formulas, conversational or formal, personal or official, religious or governmental, fill a social expectation.

The poet offers something similar to what the conventional phrases might do, sometimes based on such phrases, but transformed. Our hunting party's arms were stronger than the limbs of a lion, says the poet, their eyes were more all-seeing than the sun at noon. Or, my love grew in my heart without warning or intention, it was a weed that broke open my chest. Or, behold, Earth is our mother, full of flowers in May, but she will devour us, in her underground which is darker than midnight in December. Or, here is a story that begins with a royal physician and ends, one thing leading to another, with acrobats, miracles, and tattoos, the sacred wedded to the profane.

Melody or chanting likely energizes the process, but the transformation is not only a matter of form or music. Something else happens: work performed by what is now called "the imagination," once known as "the fancy"—a faculty traditionally associated with dreaming. In the psychological theory of Sigmund Freud and also in an ancient psychological tradition, desire and the imagination are closely related to dreams. In both the ancient and modern psychologies, dreams reveal or express feelings not available in waking life.

Remarkably, in the ancient tradition, the imagination or "phantasy" was considered a sense. In that psychology, in the detailed summary of Robert Burton's 1620 *Anatomy of Melancholy*, in addition to the outward senses of sight, hearing, smell, taste, and touch, we have three inward senses: the Common Sense, Memory, and Phantasy.

The Common Sense organizes the particulars perceived by our outward senses: in Burton's words: "This common sense is the judge or moderator of the rest, by whom we discern all differences of objects; for by mine eye I know not that I see, or by mine ear that I hear, but by my common sense." Memory retains what is perceived by the other senses. Then, says Burton:

Phantasy, or imagination . . . is an inward sense which doth more fully examine the species perceived by common sense, of things present or absent, and keeps them longer, recalling them to mind again or making new of his own. In time of sleep this faculty is free, and many times conceives strange, stupend, absurd shapes, as in sick men we commonly observe. . . . his objects all the species communicated to him by the common sense, by comparison of which he feigns infinite others to himself. In melancholy men this faculty is most powerful and strong, and often hurts, producing many monstrous and prodigious things, especially if it be stirred up by some terrible object . . . from common sense or memory. In Poets and

Painters imagination forcibly works, as appears by their several fictions, anticks, images: as Ovid's House of Sleep, Psyche's Palace in Apuleius, &c.

Questions about the nature of poetry, or poetics, are endless—and worth pondering. And it is worth including in the mix this old idea of imagination as a sense, that produces "monstrous and prodigious things" by recombining and re-forming the more orderly perceptions of memory and the other senses. As in dreams, the ingredients are familiar but the new reality is not. Even apparently plain, straightforward language can have the quality of imaginative transformation. There is a dreamlike fitness and mystery in the unadorned sentence:

Saul and Jonathan were lovely and pleasant in their lives, and in their death they were not divided.

Somewhere in the process of composition in Hebrew and sixteenth-century translation into English, imagination put the pair "lovely and pleasant" before "death" and "divided." Without images or striking figures of speech, the words are haunting, changing and changed by the two conventional similes that come next:

They were swifter than eagles, they were stronger than lions.

As in Homeric epic poetry, the formulaic nature of these similes becomes part of the dignity and scale: timeless, rather than trite. In dreams, too, ordinary phrases and images can acquire tremendous meaning and importance, in a compressed interaction of context and mystery.

The old, premodern psychology Burton summarizes has its limits. Imagination is more than an inward sense. It is both a way of seeing reality and a source of new realities, though combining the two—seeing what *is* and making what *was not*—may suggest a contradiction. Possibly the most celebrated formulation about this modern, double function of imagination is Marianne Moore's "'imaginary gardens with real toads in them'" in her poem "Poetry" (p. 194). As a kind of oblique tribute to how complex the duality is, Moore puts her formulation in quotation marks—suggesting that the memorable phrase about gardens and toads were something she read somewhere, although it seems that she made it up, using some imaginative punctuation to step away from it, just a bit.

Part of making a poem—does this need saying?—is a process of daydreaming. All technical concerns and challenges are useful, ultimately, as ways to stimulate the essential creative work of dreaming up something new. In his brief essay "On Creative Writers and Daydreaming," Freud says of "the relation of fantasies to dreams":

> Our dreams at night are nothing else than fantasies like these, as we can demonstrate from the interpretation of dreams. Language, in its unrivaled wisdom, long ago decided the question of the essential nature of dreams by giving the name of *daydreams* to the airy creations of fantasy.

The dream, the daydream, the poem as it begins developing in the poet's imagination and voice, all share an essential quality: authority. No matter how bizarre or irrational the peculiar rules, they are accepted as a fact, akin to the force of gravity in the ordinary, waking world. Dante in the *Inferno* pauses to address the reader, almost apologetically, before he proceeds to describe the shade of a fellow-poet, Bertrand de Born, carrying his severed head in one hand like a lantern as he strides in Hell:

> I stayed to see more, one sight so incredible
>   As I should fear to describe, except that conscience,
>   Being pure in this, encourages me to tell:

I saw—and writing it now, my brain still envisions—
   A headless trunk that walked, in sad promenade
   Shuffling the dolorous track with its companions,

And the trunk was carrying the severed head,
   Gripping its hair like a lantern, letting it swing,
   And the head looked up at us: "Oh me!" it cried.

The circumstantial details ("letting it swing") are reenforced by
the authority of this created, dreamed-up scene: the poet is reluc-
tant to tell what he saw, but he is conscience-bound to tell it.
That is a kind of serious joke about imaginative reality.

   With similar components but a different tone, Elizabeth
Bishop begins "The Weed" (p. 154) with an impossibility in the
first line: the contradiction, between "dead" and "meditating."
As in the *Inferno* passage, there are circumstantial details, and
something like the poet's suppressed laugh of astonishment at
the authority of her own imagination. Parallel to Dante's sup-
posed reluctance to describe the headless walker, a hesitation he
claims has been overcome by a conscience-impelled requirement
that he report the facts, Bishop's surface is careful, reportorial in
tone, unastonished:

I dreamed that dead, and meditating,
I lay upon a grave, or bed,
(at least, some cold and close-built bower).
In the cold heart, its final thought
Stood frozen, drawn immense and clear,
stiff and idle as I was there;
and we remained unchanged together
for a year, a minute, an hour.

The ineffable authority of dream-power, central to the art of
poetry, is celebrated in Shakespeare's famous speech for Bottom
the Weaver in *A Midsummer Night's Dream*. The comic amaze-
ment at the dream energy here is explicit, as the examples from

Dante and Bishop are not. As in those examples, death too is incorporated by the unfathomable power of imagination:

> I have had a most rare vision. I have had a dream, past the wit of man to say what dream it was: man is but an ass, if he go about to expound this dream. Methought I was— there is no man can tell what. Methought I was, and methought I had, but man is but a patched fool, if he will offer to say what methought I had. The eye of man hath not heard, the ear of man hath not seen, man's hand is not able to taste, his tongue to conceive, nor his heart to report, what my dream was. I will get Peter Quince to write a ballad of this dream: it shall be called Bottom's Dream, because it hath no bottom; and I will sing it in the latter end of a play, before the duke: peradventure, to make it the more gracious, I shall sing it at her death.

Bottom's arriving, in a comic and moving way, with "I shall sing it at her death" is a reminder that in Burton's premodern psychology Memory, too, is an inward sense. Along with Common Sense (which gathers the five senses into one coherent perception) and Fancy (which makes "strange, stupend, absurd shapes"), Memory looks inward, and it can perceive mortality.

Imagination in a work of art transforms Memory, too: not necessarily by distorting it, but by seeing it anew. What interests Thomas Hardy, in "The Self-Unseeing" (p. 160), is the unaware-ness of the present as it slips into the past: retrospectively, in memory transformed by imagination, the moment attains a new level of reality, vivid though melancholy:

THE SELF-UNSEEING

Here is the ancient floor,
Footworn and hollow and thin,
Here was the former door
Where the dead feet walked in.

She sat here in her chair,
Smiling into the fire;
He who played stood there,
Bowing it higher and higher.

Childlike, I danced in a dream;
Blessings emblazoned that day;
Everything glowed with a gleam;
Yet we were looking away!

In the footworn threshold and the ancient floor, in the daring
passage "Here was the former door / Where the dead feet
walked in," Hardy demonstrates the perceptions of the outward
senses and memory, along with the poetic imagination that is
faithful to those perceptions, even as it transfigures them.

Transfiguration, in all its forms, is everything.

ELIZABETH BISHOP, "The Weed"

For an anthology in which living poets each selected one historic poem and one of their own related to it, Bishop chose George Herbert's "Love Unknown" and her "The Weed." The principle she invoked was writing about the fantastic in a plain, pure way, as though it were something that happened yesterday. The more fantastic the material, the more straightforward the language.

The Weed

I dreamed that dead, and meditating,
I lay upon a grave, or bed,
(at least, some cold and close-built bower).
In the cold heart, its final thought
stood frozen, drawn immense and clear,
stiff and idle as I was there;
and we remained unchanged together
for a year, a minute, an hour.
Suddenly there was a motion,
as startling, there, to every sense
as an explosion. Then it dropped
to insistent, cautious creeping
in the region of the heart,
prodding me from desperate sleep.
I raised my head. A slight young weed
had pushed up through the heart and its
green head was nodding on the breast.
(All this was in the dark.)
It grew an inch like a blade of grass;
next, one leaf shot out of its side
a twisting, waving flag, and then
two leaves moved like a semaphore.

The stem grew thick. The nervous roots
reached to each side; the graceful head
changed its position mysteriously,
since there was neither sun nor moon
to catch its young attention.
The rooted heart began to change
(not beat) and then it split apart
and from it broke a flood of water.
Two rivers glanced off from the sides,
one to the right, one to the left,
two rushing, half-clear streams,
(the ribs made of them two cascades)
which assuredly, smooth as glass,
went off through the fine black grains of earth.
The weed was almost swept away;
it struggled with its leaves,
lifting them fringed with heavy drops.
A few drops fell upon my face
and in my eyes, so I could see
(or, in that black place, thought I saw)
that each drop contained a light,
a small, illuminated scene;
the weed-deflected stream was made
itself of racing images.
(As if a river should carry all
the scenes that it had once reflected
shut in its waters, and not floating
on momentary surfaces.)
The weed stood in the severed heart.
"What are you doing there?" I asked.
It lifted its head all dripping wet
(with my own thoughts?)
and answered then: "I grow," it said,
"but to divide your heart again."

Bishop's comparison or predecessor for "The Weed."

Love Unknown

Dear Friend, sit down, the tale is long and sad:
And in my faintings I presume your love
Will more comply, than help. A Lord I had,
And have, of whom some grounds which may improve,
I hold for two lives, and both lives in me.
To him I brought a dish of fruit one day,
And in the middle placed my heart. But he
                    (I sigh to say)
Looked on a servant, who did know his eye
Better than you know me, or (which is one)
Than I myself. The servant instantly
Quitting the fruit, seized on my heart alone,
And threw it in a font, wherein did fall
A stream of blood, which issued from the side
Of a great rock: I well remember all,
And have good cause: there it was dipped and dyed,
And washed, and wrung: the very wringing yet
Enforceth tears. *Your heart was foul, I fear.*
Indeed 'tis true. I did and do commit
Many a fault more than my lease will bear;
Yet still asked pardon, and was not denied.
But you shall hear. After my heart was well,
And clean and fair, as I one even-tide
                    (I sigh to tell)
Walked by myself abroad, I saw a large
And spacious furnace flaming, and thereon
A boiling cauldron, round about whose verge
Was in great letters set AFFLICTION.

The greatness showed the owner. So I went
To fetch a sacrifice out of my fold,
Thinking with that, which I did thus present,
To warm his love, which I did fear grew cold.
But as my heart did tender it, the man
Who was to take it from me, slipped his hand,
And threw my heart into the scalding pan;
My heart, that brought it (do you understand?)
The offerer's heart. *Your heart was hard, I fear.*
Indeed 'tis true. I found a callous matter
Began to spread and to expatiate there:
But with a richer drug than scalding water,
I bathed it often, ev'n with holy blood,
Which at a board, while many drunk bare wine,
A friend did steal into my cup for good,
Ev'n taken inwardly, and most divine
To supple hardnesses. But at the length
Out of the cauldron getting, soon I fled
Unto my house, where to repair the strength
Which I had lost, I hasted to my bed.
But when I thought to sleep out all these faults
                    (I sigh to speak)
I found that some had stuffed the bed with thoughts,
I would say *thorns.* Dear, could my heart not break,
When with my pleasures ev'n my rest was gone?
Full well I understood, who had been there:
For I had giv'n the key to none, but one:
It must be he. *Your heart was dull, I fear.*
Indeed a slack and sleepy state of mind
Did oft posses me, so that when I prayed,
Though my lips went, my heart did stay behind.
But all my scores were by another paid,
Who took the debt upon him. *Truly, Friend,*
For ought I hear, your Master shows to you
More favour than you wot of. Mark the end.

The Font did only, what was old, renew:
The Cauldron suppled, what was grown too hard:
The Thorns did quicken, what was grown too dull:
All did but strive to mend, what you had marred.
Wherefore be cheered, and praise him to the full
Each day, each hour, each moment of the week,
Who fain would have you be, new, tender, quick.

*Surrealists can try, but nothing is more arrestingly, powerfully
weird than the work of this Jesuit martyr and saint.*

The Burning Babe

As I in hoary winter's night stood shivering in the snow,
Surprised I was with sudden heat which made my heart to
    glow;
And lifting up a fearful eye to view what fire was near,
A pretty babe all burning bright did in the air appear;
Who, scorched with excessive heat, such floods of tears did
    shed
As though his floods should quench his flames which with his
    tears were fed.
"Alas," quoth he, "but newly born in fiery heats I fry,
Yet none approach to warm their hearts or feel my fire but I!
My faultless breast the furnace is, the fuel wounding thorns,
Love is the fire, and sighs the smoke, the ashes shame and
    scorns;
The fuel justice layeth on, and mercy blows the coals,
The metal in this furnace wrought are men's defilèd souls,
For which, as now on fire I am to work them to their good,
So will I melt into a bath to wash them in my blood."
With this he vanished out of sight and swiftly shrunk away,
And straight I callèd unto mind that it was Christmas day.

The dream is a present moment, the reality is dead feet walking.

The Self-Unseeing

Here is the ancient floor,
Footworn and hollowed and thin,
Here was the former door
Where the dead feet walked in.

She sat here in her chair,
Smiling into the fire;
He who played stood there,
Bowing it higher and higher.

Childlike, I danced in a dream;
Blessings emblazoned that day;
Everything glowed with a gleam;
Yet we were looking away!

Could this poem have inspired the mutilated knight played by John Cleese in Monty Python and the Holy Grail, *who says of a severed limb, "It's just a flesh wound"? Ransom dreams up the credulous, naïve balladeer who tells the story. The invention of that narrator somehow lets the poem be both comical and moving.*

Captain Carpenter

Captain Carpenter rose up in his prime
Put on his pistols and went riding out
But had got wellnigh nowhere at that time
Till he fell in with ladies in a rout.

It was a pretty lady and all her train
That played with him so sweetly but before
An hour she'd taken a sword with all her main
And twined him of his nose for evermore.

Captain Carpenter mounted up one day
And rode straightway into a stranger rogue
That looked unchristian but be that as may
The Captain did not wait upon prologue.

But drew upon him out of his great heart
The other swung against him with a club
And cracked his two legs at the shinny part
And let him roll and stick like any tub.

Captain Carpenter rode many a time
From male and female took he sundry harms
He met the wife of Satan crying "I'm
The she-wolf bids you shall bear no more arms."

Their strokes and counters whistled in the wind
I wish he had delivered half his blows
But where she should have made off like a hind
The bitch bit off his arms at the elbows.

And Captain Carpenter parted with his ears
To a black devil that used him in this wise
O Jesus ere his threescore and ten years
Another had plucked out his sweet blue eyes.

Captain Carpenter got up on his roan
And sallied from the gate in hell's despite
I heard him asking in the grimmest tone
If any enemy yet there was to fight?

"To any adversary it is fame
If he risk to be wounded by my tongue
Or burnt in two beneath my red heart's flame
Such are the perils he is cast among.

"But if he can he has a pretty choice
From an anatomy with little to lose
Whether he cut my tongue and take my voice
Or whether it be my round red heart he choose."

It was the neatest knave that ever was seen
Stepping in perfume from his lady's bower
Who at this word put in his merry mien
And fell on Captain Carpenter like a tower.

I would not knock old fellows in the dust
But there lay Captain Carpenter on his back
His weapons were the old heart in his bust
And a blade shook between rotten teeth alack.

The rogue in scarlet and grey soon knew his mind
He wished to get his trophy and depart
With gentle apology and touch refined
He pierced him and produced the Captain's heart.

God's mercy rest on Captain Carpenter now
I thought him Sirs an honest gentleman
Citizen husband soldier and scholar enow
Let jangling kites eat of him if they can.

But God's deep curses follow after those
That shore him of his goodly nose and ears
His legs and strong arms at the two elbows
And eyes that had not watered seventy years.

The curse of hell upon the sleek upstart
That got the Captain finally on his back
And took the red red vitals of his heart
And made the kites to whet their beaks clack clack.

JORGE DE LIMA, "The Big Mystical Circus"
(translated by Dudley Poore)

An imagination-show that turns out to be truly large in feeling.
The implied assignment might be to set a narrative spinning,
and let it roam like a top on a hard surface.

The Big Mystical Circus

Frederick Knieps, Physician of the Bed-Chamber to the
    Empress Theresa,
resolved that his son also should be a doctor,
but the youth, having established relations with Agnes, the
    tightrope artist,
married her and founded the circus dynasty of Knieps
with which the newspapers are so much concerned.
Charlotte, the daughter of Frederick, married the clown,
Whence sprang Marie and Otto.
Otto married Lily Braun, the celebrated contortionist,
who had a saint's image tattooed on her belly.
The daughter of Lily Braun—she of the tattooed belly—
wanted to enter a convent,
but Otto Frederick Knieps would not consent,
and Margaret continued the circus dynasty
with which the newspapers are so much concerned.
Then Margaret had her body tattooed,
suffering greatly for the love of God,
and caused to be engraved on her rosy skin
the Fourteen Stations of our Lord's Passion.
No tiger ever attacked her;
the lion Nero, who had already eaten two ventriloquists,
when she entered his cage nude,
wept like a new-born babe.

Her husband, the trapeze artist Ludwig, never could love her
     thereafter,
because the sacred engravings obliterated
both her skin and his desire.
Then the pugilist Rudolph, who was an atheist
and a cruel man, attacked Margaret and violated her.
After this, he was converted and died.
Margaret bore two daughters who are the wonder of Knieps'
     Great Circus.
But the greatest of miracles is their virginity,
against which bankers and gentlemen with monocles beat in
     vain:
their levitations, which the audience thinks a fraud;
their chastity, in which nobody believes;
their magic, which the simple-minded say is the devil's;
yet the children believe in them, are their faithful followers,
     their friends, their devoted worshipers.
Marie and Helène perform nude;
they dance on the wire and so dislocate their limbs
that their arms and legs no longer appear their own.
The spectators shout encore to thighs, encore to breasts, encore
     to armpits.
Marie and Helène give themselves wholly,
and are shared by cynical men;
but their souls, which nobody sees, they keep pure.
And when they display their limbs in the sight of men,
They display their souls in the sight of God.
With the true history of Knieps' Great Circus
the newspapers are very little concerned.

ROBERT HERRICK, "The Shooe Tying" and
"To God, on His Sicknesse"

*One person's imagination is capable of surprise and variety,
but in another way each imagination is unique as our finger-
prints and retinas.*

The Shooe Tying

Anthea bade me tye her shooe;
I did; and kist the Instep too:
And would have kist unto her knee,
Had not her Blush rebuked me.

To God, on His Sicknesse

What though my Harp, and Violl be
Both hung upon the Willow-tree?
What though my bed be now my grave,
And for my house I darknesse have?
What though my healthfull dayes are fled,
And I lie numbred with the dead?
Yet I have hope, by Thy great power,
To spring; though now a wither'd flower.

Mother Earth devours us her children and our "crisp knowl-
edge." The creation of the final image and its language is
amazing—the kind of imaginative stroke that cannot be forced
or willed, I think. A lightning stroke, though in this case a
stroke of darkness, or amid darkness.

Madame La Fleurie

Weight him down, O side-stars, with the great weightings of
    the end.
Seal him there. He looked in a glass of the earth and thought he
    lived in it.
Now, he brings all that he saw into the earth, to the waiting
    parent.
His crisp knowledge is devoured by her, beneath a dew.

Weight him, weight, weight him with the sleepiness of the
    moon.
It was only a glass because he looked in it. It was nothing he
    could be told.
It was a language he spoke, because he must, yet did not know.
It was a page he had found in the handbook of heartbreak.

The black fugatos are strumming the blacknesses of black . . .
The thick strings stutter the finial gutturals.
He does not lie there remembering the blue-jay, say the jay.
His grief is that his mother should feed on him, himself and
    what he saw,
In that distant chamber, a bearded queen, wicked in her dead
    light.

There is a place where sincerity meets invention. Hard to doubt that this pet existed, and that Cowper was fond of it. To create this degree and kind of directness takes an immense effort of imagination.

Epitaph on a Hare

Here lies, whom hound did ne'er pursue,
    Nor swifter greyhound follow,
Whose foot ne'er tainted morning dew,
    Nor ear heard huntsman's hallo',

Old Tiney, surliest of his kind,
    Who, nursed with tender care,
And to domestic bounds confined,
    Was still a wild jack-hare.

Though duly from my hand he took
    His pittance every night,
He did it with a jealous look,
    And, when he could, would bite.

His diet was of wheaten bread,
    And milk, and oats, and straw,
Thistles, or lettuces instead,
    With sand to scour his maw.

On twigs of hawthorn he regaled,
    On pippins russet peel;
And, when his juicy salads failed,
    Sliced carrot pleased him well.

A Turkey carpet was his lawn,
    Whereon he loved to bound,
To skip and gambol like a fawn,
    And swing his rump around.

His frisking was at evening hours,
    For then he lost his fear;
But most before approaching showers,
    Or when a storm drew near.

Eight years and five round-rolling moons
    He thus saw steal away,
Dozing out all his idle noons,
    And every night at play.

I kept him for his humor's sake,
    For he would oft beguile
My heart of thoughts that made it ache,
    And force me to a smile.

But now, beneath this walnut-shade
    He finds his long, last home,
And waits in snug concealment laid,
    Till gentler Puss shall come.

He, still more agèd, feels the shocks
    From which no care can save,
And, partner once of Tiney's box,
    Must soon partake his grave.

LOUISE BOGAN, "Women"

What assignment might she have given herself, fulfilled by this poem?

Women

Women have no wilderness in them,
They are provident instead,
Content in the tight hot cell of their hearts
To eat dusty bread.

They do not see cattle cropping red winter grass.
They do not hear
Snow water going down under culverts
Shallow and clear.

They wait, when they should turn to journeys.
They stiffen, when they should bend.
They use against themselves that benevolence
To which no man is friend.

They cannot think of so many crops to a field
Or of clean wood cleft by an axe.
Their love is an eager meaninglessness
Too tense, or too lax.

They hear in every whisper that speaks to them
A shout and a cry.
As like as not, when they take life over their door-sills
They should let it go by.

All of those old movies in which ethnic stereotypes, especially beaming black people, admire the young white and Anglo lovers: Brown simply flips that convention, without fuss. He transforms the aggressive lexicon of "Mick" and "Dago" into the lush texture of a New York transformed by love. Shocking and brilliant.

Harlem Happiness

I think there is in this the stuff for many lyrics:—
A dago fruit stand at three A.M.; the wop asleep, his woman
Knitting a tiny garment, laughing when we approached her,
Flashing a smile from white teeth, then weighing out the
    grapes,
Grapes large as plums, and tart and sweet as—well we know
    the lady
And purplish red and firm, quite as this lady's lips are. . . .
We laughed, all three when she awoke her swarthy, snoring
    Pietro
To make us change, which we, rich paupers, left to help the
    garment.
We swaggered off; while they two stared, and laughed in
    understanding,
And thanked us lovers who brought back an old Etrurian
    springtide.
Then, once beyond their light, a step beyond their pearly
    smiling
We tasted grapes and tasted lips, and laughed at sleepy Harlem,
And when the huge Mick cop stomped by, a'swingin' of his billy
You nodded to him gaily, and I kissed you with him looking,
Beneath the swinging light that weakly fought against the mist
That settled on Eighth Avenue, and curled around the houses.

And he grinned too and understood the wisdom of our
    madness.
That night at least the world was ours to spend, nor were we
    misers.
Ah, Morningside with Maytime awhispering in the foliage!
Alone, atop the city,—the tramps were still in shelter—
And moralizing lights that peered up from the murky distance
Seemed soft as our two cigarette ends burning slowly, dimly,
And careless as the jade stars that winked upon our
    gladness. . . .

And when I flicked my cigarette, and we watched it falling,
    falling,
It seemed a shooting meteor, that we, most proud creators
Sent down in gay capriciousness upon a trivial Harlem—

And then I madly quoted lyrics from old kindred masters,
Who wrote of you, unknowing you, for far more lucky me—
And you sang broken bits of song, and we both slept in
    snatches,
And so the night sped on too swift, with grapes, and words and
    kisses,
And numberless cigarette ends glowing in the darkness
Old Harlem slept regardless, but a motherly old moon—
Shone down benevolently on two happy wastrel lovers. . . .

ELIZABETH I, "When I Was Fair and Young"

Authorship, uncertain, debated by scholars. What's interesting is that a head of state had an education that makes her authorship possibly genuine.

When I Was Fair and Young

When I was fair and young, then favor graced me.
Of many was I sought their mistress for to be,
But I did scorn them all and answered them therefore:
Go, go, go, seek some other where, importune me no more.

How many weeping eyes I made to pine in woe,
How many sighing hearts I have not skill to show,
But I the prouder grew and still this spake therefore:
Go, go, go, seek some other where, importune me no more.

Then spake fair Venus' son, that proud victorious boy,
Saying: You dainty dame, for that you be so coy,
I will so pluck your plumes as you shall say no more:
Go, go, go, seek some other where, importune me no more.

As soon as he had said, such change grew in my breast
That neither night nor day I could take any rest.
Wherefore I did repent that I had said before:
Go, go, go, seek some other where, importune me no more.

WALT WHITMAN, "Vigil Strange I Kept on the Field
   One Night"

*Dream and reality, horror and love, the anonymity of Civil
War dead and the second-person poem: here is a great imagi-
nation wandering among boundaries, ardently engaging them
and crossing them. Does the story feel real? Does that matter?*

Vigil Strange I Kept on the Field One Night

Vigil strange I kept on the field one night;
When you my son and my comrade dropt at my side that day,
One look I but gave which your dear eyes return'd with a look I
   shall never forget,
One touch of your hand to mine O boy, reach'd up as you lay
   on the ground,
Then onward I sped in the battle, the even-contested battle,
Till late in the night reliev'd to the place at last again I made my
   way,
Found you in death so cold dear comrade, found your body son
   of responding kisses, (never again on earth responding,)
Bared your face in the starlight, curious the scene, cool blew the
   moderate night-wind,
Long there and then in vigil I stood, dimly around me the
   battle-field spreading,
Vigil wondrous and vigil sweet there in the fragrant silent
   night,
But not a tear fell, not even a long-drawn sigh, long, long I
   gazed,
Then on the earth partially reclining sat by your side leaning
   my chin in my hands,
Passing sweet hours, immortal and mystic hours with you
   dearest comrade—not a tear, not a word,

Vigil of silence, love and death, vigil for you my son and my
  soldier,
As onward silently stars aloft, eastward new ones upward stole,
Vigil final for you brave boy, (I could not save you, swift was
  your death,
I faithfully loved you and cared for you living, I think we shall
  surely meet again,)
Till at latest lingering of the night, indeed just as the dawn
  appear'd,
My comrade I wrapt in his blanket, envelop'd well his form,
Folded the blanket well, tucking it carefully over head and
  carefully under feet,
And there and then and bathed by the rising sun, my son in his
  grave, in his rude-dug grave I deposited,
Ending my vigil strange with that, vigil of night and battle-field
  dim,
Vigil for boy of responding kisses, (never again on earth
  responding,)
Vigil for comrade swiftly slain, vigil I never forget, how as day
  brighten'd,
I rose from the chill ground and folded my soldier well in his
  blanket,
And buried him where he fell.

SYLVIA PLATH, "Nick and the Candlestick"

Take a look at this poem among the videos at www.favorite poem.org. The man who reads the poem says "it does not proceed rationally." Assuming he is right, how does it proceed? Could you write a poem that proceeds that way?

Nick and the Candlestick

I am a miner. The light burns blue.
Waxy stalactites
Drip and thicken, tears

The earthen womb
Exudes from its dead boredom.
Black bat airs

Wrap me, raggy shawls,
Cold homicides.
They weld to me like plums.

Old cave of calcium
Icicles, old echoer.
Even the newts are white,

Those holy Joes.
And the fish, the fish—
Christ! they are panes of ice,

A vice of knives,
A piranha
Religion, drinking

Its first communion out of my live toes.
The candle
Gulps and recovers its small altitude,

Its yellows hearten.
O love, how did you get here?
O embryo

Remembering, even in sleep,
Your crossed position.
The blood blooms clean

In you, ruby.
The pain
You wake to is not yours.

Love, love,
I have hung our cave with roses,
With soft rugs—

The last of Victoriana.
Let the stars
Plummet to their dark address,

Let the mercuric
Atoms that cripple drip
Into the terrible well,

You are the one
Solid the spaces lean on, envious.
You are the baby in the barn.

Lots of scholarly and literary-critical ink has reached the altar of this poem, a work of art that illustrates a fundamental truth: if you are having a good time, you don't necessarily need to know exactly where you are. Not knowing can be part of the pleasure and illumination. The language dances.

The Phoenix and the Turtle

Let the bird of loudest lay,
On the sole Arabian tree,
Herald sad and trumpet be,
To whose sound chaste wings obey.

But thou, shrieking harbinger,
Foul precurrer of the fiend,
Augur of the fever's end,
To this troop come thou not near.

From this session interdict
Every fowl of tyrant wing,
Save the eagle, feath'red king:
Keep the obsequy so strict.

Let the priest in surplice white,
That defunctive music can,
Be the death-divining swan,
Lest the requiem lack his right.

And thou treble-dated crow,
That thy sable gender mak'st
With the breath thou giv'st and tak'st,
'Mongst our mourners shalt thou go.

Here the anthem doth commence:
Love and constancy is dead;
Phoenix and the turtle fled
In a mutual flame from hence.

So they loved, as love in twain
Had the essence but in one:
Two distincts, division none;
Number there in love was slain.

Hearts remote, yet not asunder;
Distance, and no space was seen
'Twixt this turtle and his queen:
But in them it were a wonder.

So between them love did shine,
That the turtle saw his right
Flaming in the phoenix' sight;
Either was the other's mine.

Property was thus appalled
That the self was not the same;
Single nature's double name
Neither two nor one was called.

Reason, in itself confounded,
Saw division grow together,
To themselves yet either neither,
Simple were so well compounded:

That it cried, How true a twain
Seemeth this concordant one!
Love hath reason, reason none,
If what parts can so remain.

Whereupon it made this threne
To the phoenix and the dove,
Co-supremes and stars of love,
As chorus to their tragic scene.

THRENOS

Beauty, truth, and rarity,
Grace in all simplicity,
Here enclosed, in cinders lie.

Death is now the phoenix' nest,
And the turtle's loyal breast
To eternity doth rest.

Leaving no posterity,
'Twas not their infirmity,
It was married chastity.

Truth may seem, but cannot be;
Beauty brag, but 'tis not she;
Truth and beauty buried be.

To this urn let those repair
That are either true or fair;
For these dead birds sigh a prayer.

BIBLE, Samuel 2, "David's Lament for Saul and Jonathan"

A complicated background: Saul has more than once tried to kill David, and David has declared himself prepared to fight on the Philistine side in the battle where these two fell. Yet he succeeds in writing a lament that is public and erotic, patriotic and intimate.

David's Lament for Saul and Jonathan

The beauty of Israel is slain upon thy high places:
How are the mighty fallen! Tell it not
In Gath, publish it not in the streets of Askelon;
Lest the daughters of the Philistines rejoice,
Lest the daughters of the uncircumcised triumph.

Ye mountains of Gilboa, let there be
No dew, neither let there be rain, upon you,
Nor fields of offerings: for there the shield of the mighty
Is vilely cast away, the shield of Saul,
As though he had not been anointed with oil.

From the blood of the slain, from the fat of the mighty,
The bow of Jonathan turned not back,
And the sword of Saul returned not empty.
Saul and Jonathan were lovely and pleasant in their lives,
And in their death they were not divided:
They were swifter than eagles, they were stronger than lions.

Ye daughters of Israel, weep over Saul,
Who clothed you in scarlet, with other delights,
Who put on ornaments of gold upon your apparel.

How are the mighty fallen in the midst of the battle!
O Jonathan, thou wast slain in thine high places.

I am distressed for thee, my brother Jonathan:
Very pleasant hast thou been unto me:
Thy love to me was wonderful, passing the love of women.

How are the mighty fallen, and the weapons of war perished!

LEWIS CARROLL, "Jabberwocky"

"Meaning" and "nonsense" are matters of degree, aspects of one thing. Language is never purely one or the other. Charles Dodgson's first version of the poem, consisting of just the first stanza, was entitled "A Stanza of Anglo-Saxon Poetry."

Jabberwocky

'Twas brillig, and the slithy toves
    Did gyre and gimble in the wabe:
All mimsy were the borogoves,
    And the mome raths outgrabe.

"Beware the Jabberwock, my son!
    The jaws that bite, the claws that catch!
Beware the Jubjub bird, and shun
    The frumious Bandersnatch!"

He took his vorpal sword in hand:
    Long time the manxome foe he sought—
So rested he by the Tumtum tree,
    And stood awhile in thought.

And, as in uffish thought he stood,
    The Jabberwock, with eyes of flame,
Came whiffling through the tulgey wood,
    And burbled as it came!

One, two! One, two! And through and through
    The vorpal blade went snicker-snack!
He left it dead, and with its head
    He went galumphing back.

"And hast thou slain the Jabberwock?
    Come to my arms, my beamish boy!
O frabjous day! Callooh! Callay!"
    He chortled in his joy.

'Twas brillig, and the slithy toves
    Did gyre and gimble in the wabe:
All mimsy were the borogoves,
    And the mome raths outgrabe.

Without the "pavements grey" the poem would not amount to much. It's about imagining, about daydreaming—it would be less interesting to merely crank the dream-machine, without situating the dreamer.

The Lake Isle of Innisfree

I will arise and go now, and go to Innisfree,
And a small cabin build there, of clay and wattles made:
Nine bean-rows will I have there, a hive for the honey-bee,
And live alone in the bee-loud glade.

And I shall have some peace there, for peace comes dropping
    slow,
Dropping from the veils of the morning to where the cricket
    sings;
There midnight's all a glimmer, and noon a purple glow,
And evening full of the linnet's wings.

I will arise and go now, for always night and day
I hear lake water lapping with low sounds by the shore;
While I stand on the roadway, or on the pavements grey,
I hear it in the deep heart's core.

All good parody is also a tribute. An imagination conceding the power of another imagination, while also noting the irrational or goofball or idiosyncratic element in that power.

The Lake Isle

O God, O Venus, O Mercury, patron of thieves,
Give me in due time, I beseech you, a little tobacco-shop,
With the little bright boxes
         piled up neatly upon the shelves
And the loose fragrant Cavendish
         and the shag,
And the bright Virginia
         loose under the bright glass cases,
And a pair of scales not too greasy,
And the whores dropping in for a word or two in passing,
For a flip word, and to tidy their hair a bit.

O God, O Venus, O Mercury, patron of thieves,
Lend me a little tobacco-shop,
         or install me in any profession
Save this damn'd profession of writing,
         where one needs one's brains all the time.

EZRA POUND, "The River-Merchant's Wife: A Letter"

Scholarly translations of the so-to-speak "original" by Li Po
(A.D. 701–762) demonstrate that Pound basically made this up.
He imagined the poem, though in some other sense it is a
translation.

The River-Merchant's Wife: A Letter

While my hair was still cut straight across my forehead
I played about the front gate, pulling flowers.
You came by on bamboo stilts, playing horse,
You walked about my seat, playing with blue plums.
And we went on living in the village of Chokan:
Two small people, without dislike or suspicion.

At fourteen I married My Lord you.
I never laughed, being bashful.
Lowering my head, I looked at the wall.
Called to, a thousand times, I never looked back.

At fifteen I stopped scowling,
I desired my dust to be mingled with yours
Forever and forever and forever.
Why should I climb the look out?

At sixteen you departed,
You went into far Ku-to-yen, by the river of swirling eddies,
And you have been gone five months.
The monkeys make sorrowful noise overhead.

You dragged your feet when you went out.
By the gate now, the moss is grown, the different mosses,
Too deep to clear them away!

The leaves fall early this autumn, in wind.
The paired butterflies are already yellow with August
Over the grass in the West garden;
They hurt me. I grow older.
If you are coming down through the narrows of the river
    Kiang,
Please let me know beforehand,
And I will come out to meet you
                  As far as Cho-fu-Sa.

JOHN MILTON, "Methought I saw my late espousèd saint"

An account of a dream, actual or imagined—and either way relying on a great imagination in the telling. Milton's blindness adds meaning to "I saw" in the first line and "my night" in the last.

Methought I saw my late espousèd saint
    Brought to me like Alcestis from the grave,
    Whom Jove's great son to her glad husband gave,
    Rescued from Death by force, though pale and faint.
Mine, as whom washed from spot of child-bed taint
    Purification in the Old Law did save,
    And such, as yet once more I trust to have
    Full sight of her in heaven without restraint,
Came vested all in white, pure as her mind.
    Her face was veiled; yet to my fancied sight
    Love, sweetness, goodness, in her person shined
So clear as in no face with more delight.
    But O, as to embrace me she inclined,
    I waked, she fled, and day brought back my night.

WILLIAM BUTLER YEATS, from "A Woman Young and Old,"
IV: "Her Triumph"

*The dragon? The seabird? They are part of the same evolution-
ary chain as the slithy toves of "Jabberwocky."*

---

from A Woman Young and Old

IV
Her Triumph

I did the dragon's will until you came
Because I had fancied love a casual
Improvisation, or a settled game
That followed if I let the kerchief fall:
Those deeds were best that gave the minute wings
And heavenly music if they gave it wit;
And then you stood among the dragon-rings.
I mocked, being crazy, but you mastered it
And broke the chain and set my ankles free,
Saint George or else a pagan Perseus;
And now we stare astonished at the sea,
And a miraculous strange bird shrieks at us.

He imagines what it would be to make song the way the bird
does and he imagines the absolute difference between himself
and the bird. "The fancy cannot cheat so well"—a comment on
the sweetness of not thinking? Can you, in the twenty-first cen-
tury, write a second-person ode without irony?

Ode to a Nightingale

1

My heart aches, and a drowsy numbness pains
    My sense, as though of hemlock I had drunk,
Or emptied some dull opiate to the drains
    One minute past, and Lethe-wards had sunk:
Tis not through envy of thy happy lot,
    But being too happy in thine happiness—
        That thou, light-wingèd Dryad of the trees,
           In some melodious plot
    Of beechen green, and shadows numberless,
        Singest of summer in full-throated ease.

2

O, for a draught of vintage! that hath been
    Cooled a long age in the deep-delvèd earth,
Tasting of Flora and the country green,
    Dance, and Provençal song, and sunburnt mirth!
O for a beaker full of the warm South,
    Full of the true, the blushful Hippocrene,
        With beaded bubbles winking at the brim,
           And purple-stainèd mouth;
    That I might drink, and leave the world unseen,
        And with thee fade away into the forest dim:

3

Fade far away, dissolve, and quite forget
   What thou among the leaves hast never known,
The weariness, the fever, and the fret
   Here, where men sit and hear each other groan;
Where palsy shakes a few, sad, last gray hairs,
     Where youth grows pale, and specter-thin, and dies,
        Where but to think is to be full of sorrow
           And leaden-eyed despairs,
     Where Beauty cannot keep her lustrous eyes,
        Or new Love pine at them beyond tomorrow.

4

Away! away! for I will fly to thee,
   Not charioted by Bacchus and his pards,
But on the viewless wings of Poesy,
   Though the dull brain perplexes and retards:
Already with thee! tender is the night,
     And haply the Queen-Moon is on her throne,
        Clustered around by all her starry Fays;
           But here there is no light,
     Save what from heaven is with the breezes blown
        Through verdurous glooms and winding mossy ways.

5

I cannot see what flowers are at my feet,
   Nor what soft incense hangs upon the boughs,
But, in embalmèd darkness, guess each sweet
   Wherewith the seasonable month endows
The grass, the thicket, and the fruit tree wild;
     White hawthorn, and the pastoral eglantine;
        Fast fading violets covered up in leaves;
           And mid-May's eldest child,
     The coming musk-rose, full of dewy wine,
        The murmurous haunt of flies on summer eves.

6

Darkling I listen; and for many a time
   I have been half in love with easeful Death,
Called him soft names in many a musèd rhyme,
   To take into the air my quiet breath;
Now more than ever seems it rich to die,
   To cease upon the midnight with no pain,
      While thou art pouring forth thy soul abroad
        In such an ecstasy!
   Still wouldst thou sing, and I have ears in vain—
      To thy high requiem become a sod.

7

Thou wast not born for death, immortal Bird!
   No hungry generations tread thee down;
The voice I hear this passing night was heard
   In ancient days by emperor and clown:
Perhaps the selfsame song that found a path
   Through the sad heart of Ruth, when, sick for home,
      She stood in tears amid the alien corn;
        The same that ofttimes hath
   Charmed magic casements, opening on the foam
      Of perilous seas, in faery lands forlorn.

8

Forlorn! the very word is like a bell
   To toll me back from thee to my sole self!
Adieu! the fancy cannot cheat so well
   As she is famed to do, deceiving elf.
Adieu! adieu! thy plaintive anthem fades
   Past the near meadows, over the still stream,
      Up the hill side; and now 'tis buried deep
        In the next valley-glades:
   Was it a vision, or a waking dream?
      Fled is that music:—Do I wake or sleep?

May the student try writing a poem with this title.

Poetry

I, too, dislike it: there are things that are important beyond all
    this fiddle. Reading it, however, with a perfect contempt for
  it, one discovers in it, after all, a place for the genuine.
        Hands that can grasp, eyes
        that can dilate, hair that can rise
            if it must, these things are important not because a

high-sounding interpretation can be put upon them but because
    they are useful. When they become so derivative as to
    become unintelligible, the same thing may be said for all of
    us, that we
        do not admire what
        we cannot understand: the bat
            holding on upside down or in quest of something to

eat, elephants pushing, a wild horse taking a roll, a tireless wolf
    under a tree, the immovable critic twitching his skin like a
    horse that feels a flea, the base-ball fan, the statistician—
        nor is it valid
            to discriminate against "business documents and

school-books"; all these phenomena are important. One must
    make a distinction however: when dragged into prominence
    by half poets, the result is not poetry, nor till the poets
    among us can be
        "literalists of
        the imagination"—above
            insolence and triviality and can present

for inspection, "imaginary gardens with real toads in them," shall
   we have it. In the meantime, if you demand on the one hand,
   the raw material of poetry in
      all its rawness and
      that which is on the other hand
         genuine, you are interested in poetry.

*A poem about reading a poem—or rather just beginning to
read it, and in translation at that. Balboa, not Cortez, gazed
at the Pacific. But what matters is the "wild surmise" of the
young poet, embarking on the "wide expanse."*

On First Looking into Chapman's Homer

Much have I traveled in the realms of gold,
    And many goodly states and kingdoms seen;
    Round many western islands have I been
Which bards in fealty to Apollo hold.
Oft of one wide expanse had I been told
    That deep-browed Homer ruled as his demesne;
    Yet did I never breathe its pure serene
Till I heard Chapman speak out loud and bold:
Then felt I like some watcher of the skies
    When a new planet swims into his ken;
Or like stout Cortez when with eagle eyes
    He stared at the Pacific—and all his men
Looked at each other with a wild surmise—
    Silent, upon a peak in Darien.

BIOGRAPHIES

Aphra Behn (1640–1689), arguably the first female professional writer, was a dramatist, poet, and writer of "amatory fiction." Her *Oroonoko*, written after visiting an English sugar-plantation colony in Venezuela, dramatized the horrors of slavery to the English public. A devoted supporter of King Charles II, she was recruited in 1666 as a political spy under the code name "Astea," a pseudonym under which she subsequently published many of her works.

Elizabeth Bishop (1911–1979) was born in Worcester, Massachusetts. Her father died when she was an infant, and her mother was institutionalized in 1916, with Bishop raised among family members in Nova Scotia and Massachusetts. While still an undergraduate at Vassar, Bishop met Marianne Moore, an important advocate and friend, and she maintained a lifelong, deep friendship with Robert Lowell. She lived for years in Brazil with Lota de Macedo Soares. Bishop published very few poems in her lifetime—fewer than ninety.

William Blake (1757–1827) was born in London. A professional engraver, Blake produced most of his best-known works, including *Songs of Innocence and Experience*, as illustrated books with hand-colored relief etchings. A contentious, unconventional figure, he was charged on one occasion for assaulting a soldier and slandering the king. In Blake's epic poem *Milton*, the poet John Milton descends from heaven to act as Blake's spiritual guide.

Louise Bogan (1897–1970) was the daughter of a paper-mill worker. She studied at Boston University for one year before dropping out.

Determined to become a writer, Bogan moved first to New York and then to Vienna to pursue her craft. She was for many years the poetry reviewer for *The New Yorker* and became the fourth Poetry Consultant to the Library of Congress. She had an intense love affair and an enduring friendship with fellow-poet Theodore Roethke.

Sterling Brown (1901–1989) was born in Washington, DC, the son of a former slave who became a professor at the Howard University Divinity School. After graduating from Williams College and earning an A.M. at Harvard University, he embarked on a long academic career at Howard University. He was a pioneer in the appreciation of African American literature and folklore, and his poetry was highly influenced by jazz, the work song, the ballad, and the blues. Among his notable students are Toni Morrison and Kwame Nkrumah.

Thomas Campion (1567–1620) was born in London and was a doctor by trade. His lasting achievements are as a poet and a composer. He composed important collections of lyrics for lute and voice and several court masques, as well as individual poems. Campion wrote a treatise, *Observations in the Art of English Poesy*, in which he argued against rhyme—of which he was a master—and for the adoption of classical, quantitative meters. This prompted a response from Samuel Daniel, his *Defense of Rhyme*.

Lewis Carroll (1832–1898) is the pseudonym of Charles Lutwidge Dodgson. A brilliant mathematician and an important photographer, Dodgson was a lecturer at Christ Church, Oxford, where he met college dean Henry Liddell and his family. In the course of a rowing trip, Dodgson entertained the Liddell children with a story that was later written out and eventually published as *Alice's Adventures in Wonderland*. That book and its companion *Through the Looking-Glass and What Alice Found There* contain many poems and commentaries on poetry.

Gregory Corso (1930–2001) was abandoned as an infant on the steps of the New York Foundling Home. He spent much of his childhood on the streets and in jails and, eventually, prison for petty crimes. Thanks to a substantial library left by a mob-boss inmate, Corso started reading the classics and writing his first poems while serving out his sentence. Soon after his release from prison, he met Allen Ginsberg, who became a major influence and advocate.

William Cowper (1731–1800) was born in Hertfordshire, where his father was a rector in the Anglican Church of St. Peter. Cowper suffered from mental agonies that resulted in prolonged depression, a suicide attempt, and treatment in an asylum. He endured a conviction that he was doomed to eternal damnation. Nevertheless, Cowper became a popular and admired poet. He also composed notable and well-known hymns, including "Light Shining Out of Darkness."

Emily Dickinson (1830–1886) was born in Amherst, Massachusetts, and educated at Amherst Academy and briefly at Mount Holyoke Female Seminary. Burdened by the deaths of family and friends, she lived a life of increasing seclusion. Though only a handful of her poems were published in her lifetime, Dickinson was prolific, writing nearly eighteen hundred poems, most of which were discovered after her death by her sister Lavinia, who made it her mission to see them published.

Alan Dugan (1923–2003) grew up in Jamaica, Queens, New York. He served in the army during World War II. In 1961, Dugan's first book of poems, laconically and characteristically entitled *Poems*, was awarded both the Pulitzer Prize and the National Book Award. Subsequent books were *Poems Two*, *Poems Three*, and so forth, culminating in *Poems Seven: New and Complete Poetry*. Unlike many poets of his generation, Dugan did not teach at a college or university. He lived on Cape Cod, where his social world included visual artists as well as writers.

Elizabeth I (1533–1603), Queen of England and Ireland from the age of twenty-five until her death, was declared illegitimate by her father, Henry VIII, after the execution of her mother, Anne Boleyn, in 1534.

Elizabeth was later restored to the line of succession. She has been credited with several poems, though attribution cannot be positive. An eloquent public speaker and correspondent, she studied with the great humanist Roger Ascham and translated works by Petrarch and Boethius.

Robert Frost (1874–1963) moved with his mother and sister from San Francisco to the mill town of Lawrence, Massachusetts, after his father's death in 1885. Summers visiting the New Hampshire farm of a great-aunt and uncle provided the setting associated with many of Frost's poems. Frost's biographer, Lawrence Thompson, was rather harsh on him. Perhaps even more damagingly, his editor Edward Connery Lathem changed the punctuation of Frost's poems in posthumous editions, making a prized book of the pre-Lathem *Complete Poems*, which also includes Frost's valuable essay "The Figure a Poem Makes."

George Gascoigne (ca. 1535–1577) produced the first comedy in English prose and the first significant work on English prosody, a still-useful essay entitled *Certain Notes of Instruction Concerning the Making of Verse of Rhyme in English*. During his time as a soldier in the Netherlands, someone published an unauthorized edition of his work, which Gascoigne later edited and published under the title *One Hundreth Sundrie Flowres*.

Allen Ginsberg (1926–1997) was the son of Louis Ginsberg, a New Jersey poet and high school English teacher who knew William Carlos Williams. Williams wrote in his introduction to Allen Ginsberg's *Howl and Other Poems*: "I never thought he'd live to grow up and write a book of poems." Counterbalancing this vision of Ginsberg as a disturbed youth is the mature man's commitment to political justice, to Buddhism, and—as his published journals demonstrate—to the craft and history of poetry.

Fulke Greville (1554–1628) came to the royal court with his friend and fellow-aristocrat Philip Sidney. Like Sidney, Greville was a man of wealth, power, and learning as well as talent. Greville, in writing about his friend, refers to Sidney as a far brighter spirit than himself— viewed by some readers as a generous overstatement. Greville's sequence of poems, *Caelica*, moves by degrees from early poems of flirtation, courtship, and love-complaint into the later poems of moral and religious preoccupations.

Thom Gunn (1929–2004) was the son of an English newspaper editor. A year after graduating from Trinity College, Cambridge, he published his first book, *Fighting Terms,* to great acclaim, and went on to receive a Stegner Fellowship at Stanford, where he worked with poet and critic Yvor Winters. He taught for many years at the University of California, Berkeley, and lived in San Francisco. The life of that city, including gay life and the AIDS epidemic, is one of his important subjects.

Thomas Hardy (1840–1928) is the rare example of a great writer in both fiction and poetry. After the harsh reception of his novel *Jude the Obscure,* Hardy stopped writing novels and wrote poetry exclusively until his death. Despite a long estrangement and unhappy marriage, Hardy's dying wish was to be interred with his first wife, but his executor insisted that he be buried at Westminster Abbey in Poet's Corner. The compromise: Hardy's heart was buried with his first wife and his ashes in Poet's Corner.

H.D. (1886–1961) was born Hilda Doolittle in Bethlehem, Pennsylvania, and raised in a Moravian community. Her father taught astronomy at the University of Pennsylvania, where as an undergraduate H.D. was courted by her classmates William Carlos Williams and Ezra Pound. She lived most of her life as an expatriate in London and Switzerland and was in psychoanalysis with Sigmund Freud. In addition to her poems, H.D. wrote translations, verse plays, and books on Shakespeare, Freud, and Pound.

George Herbert (1593–1633) was born into an aristocratic family with literary ties—John Donne dedicated his Holy Sonnets to Herbert's mother, his patron. As a student, Herbert intended to enter the Anglican priesthood, but his abilities brought him to the attention of the king, who awarded Herbert a seat in Parliament. After the king's death, Herbert was at last free to take orders and spent the rest of his life as a rector in a small parish. His book manuscript "The Temple" was published after his death.

Robert Herrick (1591–1674) was the son of a goldsmith who died, probably by suicide, when the poet was an infant. Apprenticed to his goldsmith uncle, Herrick abandoned the trade to matriculate at St. John's College, Oxford. He entered the clergy, serving as a vicar in Devon, where he wrote many of his more than 2,500 verses—on topics ranging from women's knees to cats to compact, graceful musings on spiritual matters. Herrick was an admirer and friend of Ben Jonson, whose work influenced his own.

Gerard Manley Hopkins (1844–1889), a convert to Catholicism, became a Jesuit in 1868. Convinced that his poetry conflicted with his life in the church, Hopkins gave up writing poems until 1875, when church authorities commissioned him to write about a shipwreck in which a group of Franciscan nuns had perished. The result was "The Wreck of the Deutschland." Hopkins' works were unknown until his friend Robert Bridges compiled a volume of them for print in 1918, long after Hopkins' death from tuberculosis at the age of forty-four.

Langston Hughes (1902–1967) was born in Joplin, Missouri, and received his B.A. from Lincoln University. In grammar school his classmates elected him class poet, a choice Hughes later attributed to the stereotype that all African Americans have rhythm. The young Hughes, who until then had never given poetry much thought, accepted the honor. He went on to become a central figure in the Harlem Renaissance.

Ben Jonson (1572–1637), playwright and poet, was for a time apprenticed to his bricklayer stepfather. He attended the Westminster School, where he studied with the great humanist William Camden. Jonson wrote a magnificent elegy for William Shakespeare. A legend says that during the "Wars of the Theatres" Shakespeare performed an amusing impression of Jonson's mannerisms. Imprisoned for killing an actor in a duel, Jonson escaped hanging thanks to an archaic law that any man able to recite in Latin could not be hanged, as having "benefit of clergy."

John Keats (1795–1821) was the son of a stableman. Apprenticed to an apothecary-surgeon, he abandoned medicine for poetry. He was befriended by the liberal poet and editor Leigh Hunt. The conservative critic John Wilson Croker, associating Keats with Hunt, wrote a famously nasty review of Keats' *Endymion*, using the term "Cockney poetry." Between 1818 and 1819, Keats wrote some of the most celebrated poems in the English language. In 1820, his health failing, he left England for Rome, where he died within a few months.

Kenneth Koch (1925–2002) began writing poetry at an early age, inspired by his admiration of Shelley and Keats. At eighteen, he served in World War II as a rifleman. After the war, at Harvard, he met John Ashbery and Frank O'Hara. Koch received his Ph.D. from Columbia, where he was a popular teacher for more than forty years. He wrote *One Thousand Avant-Garde Plays*, which parodied avant-garde pretension. A recurring character in Frank O'Hara's poems, "excitement-prone Kenneth Koch" is also known for his work in poetry education for children.

Walter Savage Landor (1775–1864) was the model for Charles Dickens' tempestuous character Boythorn in *Bleak House*. A radical anti-monarchist, Landor was rusticated from Trinity College, Oxford, after firing a shot through the window of a Tory student he considered too noisy. He volunteered in the Napoleonic Wars, endured a stormy marriage ending in separation, engaged in lawsuits, and befriended William Wordsworth, Ralph Waldo Emerson, Robert and Elizabeth Barrett Browning, Thomas Carlyle, and Dickens.

Jorge de Lima (1893–1953) was a Brazilian politician, medical doctor, painter, and writer, perhaps best known for his novels. He spent some of his childhood years in Mexico. Partly African by descent (one Web site describes him—in English translation from the Portuguese—as "the many-faceted mulato from the Northeast"), de Lima was an imaginative, sophisticated modernist interested in folklore, dialects, and Afro-Brazilian culture, including the history of slavery.

Mina Loy (1882–1966), born in London, left home at seventeen to study painting in Paris, where at Gertrude and Leo Stein's salon she met Pablo Picasso, Henri Rousseau, and Guillaume Apollinaire. In Florence, Loy befriended the Futurist poet Filippo Marinetti. Her *Feminist Manifesto* (1918) responds to Marinetti's misogynist and Fascist ideology. In New York, Loy became a figure in Greenwich Village's circle of artists and writers, including Man Ray, William Carlos Williams, Marcel Duchamp, and Marianne Moore.

Andrew Marvell (1621–1678) entered Trinity College, Cambridge, at the age of twelve, and at sixteen he published two poems—one in Latin and one in Greek. Marvell's close friend John Milton helped him secure a post as Latin secretary to Cromwell's Council of State, after which he was elected to Parliament, remaining in office even after the monarchy was restored. In a reciprocal act of friendship, Marvell helped persuade the reinstated government not to execute Milton.

Michelangelo di Lodovico Buonarroti Simoni (1475–1564) was a sculptor, painter, architect, and poet. A supreme visual artist, Michelangelo viewed himself primarily as a sculptor. He created both his *David* and his *Pietá* before he was thirty. Michelangelo wrote hundreds of poems, including a sequence of love poems to a much younger man. Poems by Michelangelo have been translated into English by William Wordsworth, Henry Wadsworth Longfellow, Ralph Waldo Emerson, and John Addington Symonds.

John Milton (1608–1674), after graduating from Oxford, sequestered himself for six years of intensive study. Fluent in multiple languages, he was appointed as the Commonwealth government's official master of foreign languages and communication. Milton's *Paradise Lost* has been called the greatest literary work in English, with its blank verse influencing generations of poets. Milton's political writings included tracts in favor of divorce and against censorship. He also wrote justifying regicide but when the monarchy was reinstated he was spared, thanks to the efforts of his friend Andrew Marvell.

Marianne Moore (1887–1972) attended Bryn Mawr and taught at the Carlisle Indian School in Pennsylvania before moving to New York with her mother, with whom she lived all her life. Moore worked at the New York Public Library, where she met Wallace Stevens and William Carlos Williams. Her first book of poems was published by H.D.—without Moore's prior knowledge—in 1921. Moore edited *The Dial* from 1924 to 1929. She was an important mentor and friend to Elizabeth Bishop.

Thomas Nashe (1567–1601) was educated at Cambridge and, like George Peele and other university wits, he appears to have lived a disorderly, contentious, and somewhat desperate life in London while writing copiously, for money, in various genres. He wrote pamphlets, historical fiction, narrative pornography, and masques. He also collaborated with Ben Jonson on a play, *The Isle of Dogs*. Nashe's best-known, most memorable poems appear in his masque *Summer's Last Will and Testament*.

Frank O'Hara (1926–1966) was a central figure of the "New York School" poets and artists of the fifties and sixties, with friends including painter Willem de Kooning and poet John Ashbery. He served in World War II as a sonarman in the South Pacific. His *Lunch Poems* (1964) includes poems written during lunch breaks while a desk clerk at the Museum of Modern Art, where he later became an assistant curator. O'Hara died at the age of forty when struck by a dune buggy on Fire Island Beach.

George Peele (1556–1596) was a wit and playwright with a reputation for reckless living. After studying at Oxford, he moved to London, surviving on the scant earnings from writing plays, pageants, and poetry. His wild personal life may be exaggerated by legend. His fluent, expressive blank verse anticipates the work of Shakespeare. Some scholars believe that parts of Shakespeare's *Titus Andronicus* were written by Peele. He is said to have died of "the pox," meaning venereal disease.

Sylvia Plath (1932–1963), born in Massachusetts, met poet Ted Hughes while on a Fulbright Scholarship in England. They married and eventually moved to the United States, where Plath attended Robert Lowell's class at Boston University. Other students included Anne Sexton. The couple returned to England and separated after Plath discovered Hughes' affair with a married friend. Plath suffered from chronic depression, and after several attempts she committed suicide. She composed twenty-six of the poems in her posthumous book *Ariel* in the last month of her life.

Ezra Pound (1885–1972) began lifelong friendships with poets H.D. and William Carlos Williams while in college. As editor, promoter, reviewer, and adviser he helped many contemporaries, notably T. S. Eliot. During World War II, from Italy, Pound made pro-Fascist, anti-Semitic radio broadcasts, urging American soldiers to desert. Indicted for treason, Pound avoided trial, and possible execution, by being committed to St. Elizabeths Hospital for the Criminally Insane. The controversial 1948 Bollingen Prize for Pound's *The Pisan Cantos* led to the prize's removal from administration by the Library of Congress.

Walter Ralegh (ca. 1554–1618), politician, soldier, poet, and explorer, was a favorite of Elizabeth I, who imprisoned him in the Tower of London on discovering his secret marriage to her lady-in-waiting. Released, he voyaged to Venezuela, seeking the city of gold. After Elizabeth's death, Ralegh was arrested for treason against King James. Released again, and again sailing to Venezuela, he looted a Spanish outpost. Spain protested, Ralegh's earlier death sentence was reinstated, and he was beheaded. While imprisoned, he wrote his *Historie of the World*.

John Crowe Ransom (1888–1974) was born in Tennessee and attended Vanderbilt. Returning from a Rhodes Scholarship at Oxford, he became a professor at Vanderbilt where he was a founding member of a literary group who called themselves "the Fugitives." They shared an interest in agrarian values of the traditional South, and in traditional formal concerns. An influential critic, Ransom coined the phrase "New Criticism."

Edwin Arlington Robinson (1869–1935) received little attention until 1902, when one of his books came into the hands of President Theodore Roosevelt, who wrote a magazine article praising it. Yvor Winters writes in his book on Robinson, "For his temerity in writing a critical article, the president was generally abused by the literary experts of the period, and Robinson's poetry was belittled by them." By 1928, Robinson had been awarded three Pulitzer Prizes.

Sappho was born in the seventh century B.C. to an aristocratic family on the Greek island of Lesbos. She was considered one of the greatest lyric poets of antiquity, but until the late nineteenth century scholars thought her poetry had been completely lost. One complete poem has been recovered, as have many fragments, some from the casings of mummies discovered in Egyptian tombs in 1914. Plato referred to her as "the Tenth Muse."

William Shakespeare (1564–1616) was born in Stratford-upon-Avon, the son of a glover. He probably received a good education at a local school. At twenty-one, he left Stratford, where his wife and children remained, seeking his fortune as a writer in London. He succeeded, becoming a shareholder, actor, and playwright for the Lord Chamberlain's Men, the most successful theatrical company of his day. He also published narrative poems, with his sonnets circulated privately. In his forties, Shakespeare retired from the theater and returned to Stratford.

James Shirley (1596–1666) was a dramatist and a poet. He was also an Anglican minister until his conversion to Catholicism, after which he became a master at St. Albans School, where he wrote his first play. He left teaching and moved to London, where he wrote tirelessly for the stage until the Puritan edict of 1642 put a hold on all dramatic productions in London.

Christopher Smart (1722–1771), while still a student at Cambridge, made Latin translations of two works by Alexander Pope, who commended the student's work in a letter. Smart was known for his satirical writing and ecstatic religious practices, reportedly praying aloud in the streets loudly enough to cause a public disturbance. In 1757 he entered St. Luke's Hospital for Lunatics as a "curable patient," remaining there until 1763. His final work was *Hymns, for the Amusement of Children.*

Florence Margaret "Stevie" Smith (1902–1971) was raised by her aunt Madge Spear, an ardent feminist with whom Smith lived all her life. Her nickname was inspired by her small stature and love of riding—Steve Donaghue was a popular English jockey. Sylvia Plath admired Smith, calling herself "a desperate Smith-addict." Smith was close friends with George Orwell, who inspired two male characters in her last novel.

Robert Southwell (1561–1595) was born in England to a Catholic family. Sent to study in France, Southwell became a Jesuit priest. Arrested while operating as a secret missionary in Protestant England, Southwell was tortured and executed. In Drummond of Hawthornden's account of conversation with Ben Jonson, Jonson is quoted as saying "that so he had written that piece of 'The Burning Babe,' he would have been content to destroy many of his."

Wallace Stevens (1879–1955) was born in Reading, Pennsylvania, and attended the New York Law School. He worked in claims at the Hartford Accident and Indemnity Company until the end of his life. Stevens composed poems on his walk to work, which was largely through a Hartford park that contained many of the natural details found in his work, such as hemlocks and peacocks. At the age of seventy-six, he was awarded the Pulitzer Prize for his *Collected Poems.*

May Swenson (1913–1989) attended Utah State University. She was the eldest of ten children in a Mormon family, with Swedish the primary language spoken at home. She worked at New Directions Press for several years, reviewing manuscripts. In an introduction to *The Complete Love Poems of May Swenson*, the poet Maxine Kumin writes, "Even after the social acceptance of homosexuality, Swenson, like her friend Elizabeth Bishop, maintained her distance from woman-identified poetry."

Jonathan Swift (1667–1745) was born in Dublin to an English family. After his studies at Trinity College, he was employed as Sir John Temple's secretary and tutor to Esther Johnson, the companion of Temple's daughter and the "Stella" of Swift's poems. Swift was a staunch supporter of Irish independence, producing many political pamphlets including the celebrated "A Modest Proposal." An anonymous edition of *Gulliver's Travels*, his most celebrated work, was published with the support of friends, including Alexander Pope.

Edward Thomas (1878–1917), after graduating from Oxford, worked to survive solely on his writing, for a time reviewing over a dozen books a week. In 1914, he met and befriended Robert Frost, then living in England, who encouraged Thomas to write poems. A year later, Thomas enlisted to fight in World War I. He was killed in action soon after arriving in France. He is memorialized in Frost's poem "To E.T."

Chidiock Tichborne (ca. 1563–1586), a Roman Catholic, was sentenced to death for his part in the failed 1586 Babington Plot to assassinate Queen Elizabeth I, a Protestant, and replace her with Mary, Queen of Scots. On the eve of his execution, he sent his wife a letter that contained his famous elegy. Tichborne and six other conspirators were eviscerated, hanged, drawn, and quartered—the customary punishment for treason.

Walt Whitman (1819–1892) finished his formal education at the age of eleven. He worked as a printer, teacher, editor, and, during the Civil War, volunteer nurse. He self-published the first edition of

Leaves of Grass in 1833, sending a copy to Ralph Waldo Emerson, who responded with a celebratory letter that Whitman had published in the *New York Tribune*, without Emerson's permission. Some early critics disparaged *Leaves of Grass* for profanity and homosexuality. The work has profoundly influenced American and world literature.

William Carlos Williams (1883–1963) was born in Rutherford, New Jersey, and attended the University of Pennsylvania, where he studied medicine and began close friendships with poets H.D. and Ezra Pound. In 1923 Williams, at his own expense, published the landmark *Spring and All*, a daring work in prose and verse that at first went largely unnoticed. His notable prose works include *In the American Grain* and *White Mule*.

John Wilmot, 2nd Earl of Rochester (1647–1680) was known for his extraordinary wit, learning, debauchery, and drunkenness. His satires of King Charles II frequently resulted in his banishment from court (and once landed him in the Tower of London), but, being prized for his charm and ability to amuse, he was just as often welcomed back again. He died at the age of thirty-three from venereal disease and alcoholism.

William Butler Yeats (1865–1939) was born in Dublin, Ireland, to an artistic Anglo-Irish family. His father and brother were both painters, and two of his sisters were artists. Yeats took part in the Celtic Revival movement, immersing himself in Irish folklore and mythology. He was involved in the formation of the Irish Literary Theatre. In his later years, he served in the Irish Senate.

ACKNOWLEDGMENTS

Students in Boston University's M.F.A. program, and before that at the University of California, Berkeley, have enhanced my understanding of poetry in ways that inform this book.

For their practical help and their wisdom, I am grateful to Rebekah Stout and Duy Doan, young poets who gave me their attention, encouragement, and advice.

PERMISSIONS

INDEX

ML   9-13